Praise for *Storytelling for Business*

"*Storytelling for Business: The Art and Science of Creating Connection in the Digital Age* is a thorough and holistic approach to maximize storytelling. Whether you are new to business or a seasoned professional, it is a thoughtful and helpful guide to make the most of your resources and opportunities."

Kathryn Dobbs
Senior Vice-President, Chief Marketing Officer
Columbus Blue Jackets

"In *Storytelling for Business: The Art and Science of Creating Connection in the Digital Age*, Rob Wozny provides a comprehensive and insightful resource for any business or leader wanting to truly understand the benefits of storytelling, creating a greater connection to their stakeholders."

Greg Loeppky
Vice President, Marketing
Price Industries Limited

"Storytelling has never been as important in business as it is right now. In my work as a fundraiser and marketer, I absolutely need to be proficient. Rob Wozny's use of catchy phrases to introduce important concepts is powerful. Learning through case studies is effective and Rob uses this technique so well in *Storytelling for Business: The Art and Science of Creating Connection in the Digital Age.* With strong usage of creative and contemporary communications principles and stories, mixed with real world evidence makes this book a real winner! *Storytelling for Business* is my go-to handbook going forward for me and my teams. I will use these learnings to connect with donors and with my corporate partners in how we present our relationship to the public."

Guy Yerama, CFRE
National Director of Leadership and Legacy Giving
The Salvation Army

"Is there anyone in the world who doesn't love a good story? What if it were possible for business owners to harness the power of storytelling to achieve their aims? Well, it is, and *Storytelling for Business: The Art and Science of Creating Connection in the Digital Age* shows you how. This is the ultimate soup-to-nuts directory on how to tell stories in winning and effective ways in today's world. Whether you're a shy introvert who cringes at the idea of self-promotion or a natural-born showboat who is ready to take centre stage, Rob Wozny's book will help you hit the right tone, at the right time, for the right audience."

Dr. Moira Somers, Ph.D., C.Psych.
Author, *Advice that Sticks: How to Give Financial Advice that People will Follow*

"Operating and owning a small business is the greatest responsibility I've ever been afforded, building a medium-sized business ($5M+ revenue/50+ employees), which seems more sustainable in reading *Storytelling for Business: The Art and Science of Creating Connection in the Digital Age.* The book is an exercise in discipline, creativity, engaging with your customers, and trusting those who can help you 'get you there'. If you're an entrepreneur, sit down, take a deep breath and do yourself a favour. Read this book. Your business deserves it."

Christian Clavelle
President
Canadian First-Aid Training Ltd.

"At the heart of every organization are remarkable stories waiting and needing to be told that can profoundly connect business with both its external and internal audiences. *Storytelling for Business: The Art and Science of Creating Connection in the Digital Age* by Rob Wozny serves as an essential conduit for any storyteller wanting to make that impactful connection."

Cindy Fuchs
Executive Director
Saskatchewan Roughrider Foundation

"Rob Wozny has taken the guesswork out of the business case for storytelling within any organization. In *Storytelling for Business, The Art and Science of Creating Connection in the Digital Age*, he takes us on a journey of the 'why' and the 'how' that will help any business executive plan for great communications and storytelling. A must read for leaders to better understand the role and value of well-planned, scalable communications, and an excellent tool to serve as a check-in for communicators."

Jennifer Rodrigue
Director of Communications and Public Affairs
St. Amant

"As a professional speaker, coach, and columnist, I am a story hunter, knowing the power of story to move listeners to action. Rob Wozny's decades of lived experience and expertise delivers a practical toolkit for actionable insights to help us as business owners be more effective in our storytelling strategies. *Storytelling for Business: The Art and Science of Creating Connection in the Digital Age* is destined to be a go-to resource to motivate us all to craft our stories with meaning and purpose. As a farm transition expert, I have seen the healing power of stories to motivate clients to action. I celebrate with Rob Wozny as his insights have now been launched in this great resource."

Elaine Froese
"Canada's Farm Whisperer"
Certified Professional Speaker (CSP), Certified Hudson Institute
Coach, Grainews Columnist, Award-winning author
150 Manitoba Women Trailblazer

"When I work with the marketing departments of various companies, I often hear people talk about communicating their 'story'. But while this corporate buzzword gets thrown around a lot, few people truly understand stories and their application to business. Rob Wozny is someone who does. His experience and deep understanding of the subject matter are apparent from the rich content he puts forth. *Storytelling For Business: The Art and Science of Creating Connection in the Digital Age* teaches you how to be more strategic and effective in crafting a company story and getting it out to the people who need to hear it. He has written a book that marketers, business owners and entrepreneurs alike can tap into to help them hone and leverage their storytelling and communication skills."

Anders Boulanger
Founder and CEO of Engagify Inc.

STORYTELLING
— for —
BUSINESS

THE ART AND SCIENCE OF
CREATING CONNECTION
IN THE DIGITAL AGE

ROB WOZNY

First published in Great Britain by
Practical Inspiration Publishing, 2022

© Rob Wozny, 2022

The moral rights of the author have been asserted

ISBN   9781788603454 (print)
         9781788603478 (epub)
         9781788603461 (mobi)

Cover design: Oyekola Sodiq Ajibola

Want to bulk-buy copies of this book for your team and colleagues? We can introduce case studies, customize the content and co-brand *Storytelling for Business* to suit your business's needs.

Please email info@practicalinspiration.com for more details.

Practical Inspiration
Publishing

MIX
Paper from
responsible sources
FSC® C013604
www.fsc.org

Table of contents

Introduction

The growing use of storytelling in business

The word "storytelling" appeared at least four times in a communications job posting I once applied for, a position I eventually successfully landed. Truth be told, I was enjoying success operating a small communications firm, and my lifestyle and mindset left me firmly believing my entrepreneurial path was the one I'd follow until "retirement", whatever that really means in this day and age. Still, "storytelling" in this enticing job posting was the most prominent noun. Curious by nature, as most storytellers are, I simply could not resist exploring a path I had previously disregarded. To this date, I'm eternally grateful I did – all because of that word: "storytelling". What was most intriguing, and encouraging, was that storytelling had perhaps finally crossed a threshold from the abstract, in my view, normally reserved for the creative types, and planted itself with credibility into the corporate lexicon as strategy to guide an organization in its quest to tell its story externally and internally.

Furthermore, I had observed in many years past that "storytelling" was part of marketing strategies that aimed to tell an organization's story to primarily market or sell products or services. Seeing storytelling now being used in business affirmed that traditional communications could benefit from the contemporary perspective of business storytelling. The art of storytelling, which I will elaborate on further in Chapter 1, is not just some kind of abstract "art" in its own right, but it has its theory just like any other practice in other professions.

Today, it is becoming increasingly common for more organizations to invest in business storytelling through content, which presents itself in many forms and platforms, as discussed further throughout *Storytelling for Business*. As we all know, every company faces greater return on investment (ROI) accountability and scrutiny when it comes to budgets, and for storytellers of business, it's no different. Why then does storytelling for business feature so prominently in the identity and strategic plans of so many organizations? It is because the science of storytelling works. It works extremely well when utilized in traditional communications tools, strategies, tactics, and planning. Business storytelling works in the effective delivery of communications and in the channels used to distribute messages, concepts, and ideas. While not always intuitive for many business storytellers, storytelling and its impact are becoming increasingly easier to measure in terms of return on investment, and even where none can be demonstrated, storytelling can provide identity and connection between a company and all those who engage with it. More to the point, *Storytelling for Business* is for businesses and leaders that want to connect with the people that matter most to the success of their organization through the power of story.

How to read *Storytelling for Business*

Storytelling for Business is designed to take you on a storytelling journey in its own right. As you read each chapter and digest the content I've shared, you will get the most out of this book if you keep in mind that the chapters connect and support each other in an intended story arc. For example, in the first few chapters, I explain the need for business storytelling, what you need to get started, and how to distribute your stories online. The next set of chapters outline who you need to tell the story of your business to and how to know if you're actually connecting with the people that matter most to your success (customers, employees, volunteers, and other stakeholders).

The last set of chapters cover what happens when a story goes sideways and what your business can do to get back on track, and the final chapter offers influential stories I've told myself over the years, which have served me in profound ways, and I hope they will for you too as you tell the stories of your business.

Suffice it to say, we all learn from past professional experience; and while I appreciate the knowledge of direct comparison, a tremendous amount of work in real-life business storytelling needs to remain confidential, a leading tenet in productive business communications. It is also a personal belief and philosophy that concepts can be most effectively communicated by not influencing a reader's perspective with real identities, which may (or may not) deflect from transferring ideas into their own business. Therefore, to reinforce learning, in each chapter, I start with, and reference often, an anonymized case study (where some details have been fictionalized) based on work I had a direct or indirect influence on, using strategies I've employed successfully on more than one occasion. I hope you find the case studies beneficial.

Every reader's experience is unique, and while I certainly don't want to excessively influence your experience with *Storytelling for Business*, I've always appreciated it when authors preface their books with "how to use" or "perspectives to keep in mind" in their introductions. With that intention I will respectfully suggest that as you read through each sentence, paragraph, and chapter, try to envision how the content of this book can support whatever story you would like to tell for your business.

1

The (growing) need
for storytelling

Case study: Storytelling for controversial content

It was time to finally rip off the proverbial "Band-Aid" and announce a policy that would be immensely unpopular with a service-oriented client I once worked with. All the research from other industries in other markets indicated the public reception and feedback would be unfavourable, but not infinite. Nonetheless, the policy had to be announced as it was tied to business continuity and keeping customers' personal information safe and secure when using the company's products and services. Without the new policy, customers were at risk. Given the outcome was almost guaranteed to be negatively perceived, as part of the communications plan, the strategy to tell their own story about the policy was included.

The tactic was a video with the leader doing a show-and-tell about why the policy was needed. We embedded a link to the video in our media release and shared on their social media. It was risky as it was an obvious attempt to tell the story first, before the media got a hold of it with their agenda. Well, the initial negative feedback that we knew would come did come, and it was intense for a few days. As hopefully anticipated, the outrage dissipated as the media moved onto other stories and the company's policy was eventually accepted on its security merit. The storytelling for this business was used to manage an intense public affairs issue and the content's influence exceeded our expectations considerably. When the media release went out, most of the media outlets embedded our video content right onto their webpage articles that covered the story, which was significant as most editorial policies eschew the use of any content not produced by their editorial teams. However, there was our video story influencing their readers, giving us our say, our way, as part of their editorial. Furthermore, the story we produced was edited for clips for radio talks shows, sharing our messages just as we intended. Our story for our business was produced to influence and inform directly to our customers through our social media channels, but the story had the same outcome with another powerful stakeholder – the media.

A look ahead

In Chapter 1, we examine the (growing) need for storytelling in companies and organizations, along with the benefits of investing in storytelling for business. The chapter offers the most important reasons why business storytelling is such a worthwhile endeavour for your business, correlated by evidence of return on investment. Had storytelling for business not grown in influence at the boardroom table, the decision to rely on content to share the news of a challenging new policy with all stakeholders, as shared in the opening case study, would have been easily dismissed.

Storytelling at the boardroom table

Over the years, the power of business storytelling has grown in influence, supported with increased resources in many companies and organizations of all sizes because leaders see it clearly works as evidenced in managing the controversial company policy I just showcased. Gone are the days of storytelling as some abstract concept as a qualitative tactic to engage with customers and stakeholders. Now, CEOs and leaders at the largest companies around the world drop the term "storytelling" as commonly as they do other go-to business terminology when describing key objectives for their business operations. Storytelling for business has never been so widely embraced as a legitimate business tool, primarily because leaders often influence the story directly, or in many cases, become the story itself (see Chapter 6, "People power"). And if leaders embrace storytelling, their internal and external stakeholders follow as well, and thus a trusted channel of communication, in good times and bad, has been formed.

The need to tell stories in business

With storytelling for business now entrenched into business strategy, fully embraced by leaders, let's now explore the need for telling stories for your business, no matter its size or scope. While admittedly subjective, based on my experience, I'm going to suggest the need for business storytelling exists on a continuum that starts with the *onset* of a story leading to a (desirable) *outcome*, and then back again, and so it goes. Along the Business Storytelling Narrative Continuum, are some "check stops" that are in sequential in the life of a story.

Culture (internal)

As you'll read in Chapter 7's audience analysis and its ranking of stakeholders, employees are right at the top. Your employees are your ambassadors. They reflect your company's values at every interaction with your customers, partners, and other stakeholders. People connect to each other through the power of storytelling. For leaders to connect with their employees, and to move the story along the storytelling continuum, spreading their reach and influence, they're going to need their employees onboard because employees also become amplifiers of the story of that business. How you communicate externally is how you communicate internally. As part of the chapter's case study policy announcement, internal messaging and tools were developed in conjunction with the external content as the company's employees were also consuming the media's coverage. Facts, stats, and policies, while important, on their own, will not be enough to inspire employees to be your proudest storytellers. They need an overarching narrative they can believe in and get behind, and it needs to have an emotional connection that's easy to remember and share. If stakeholders want more, the technical details "for more information" can and should be always posted online on a company webpage.

Culture (external)

A company's success is the success of those who have come along for the ride, so to speak – your customers and partners who have long supported your business, and who are also powerful amplifiers of your story externally. And, if an organization's rallying cry is successful and fully accepted by its stakeholders, it can transcend from external to internal or vice versa. I'm sure many examples come to mind for you, and for me, I think of airlines like Southwest (US) and WestJet (Canada) that empower their employees as owners. With sky-high pride, they become storytellers in the companies' storytelling and on the job.

Community

Your customers have choices, and more than ever, they can find them online. They're doing their research before they engage with your business or purchase your products and services, and now more than ever, what significantly influences their purchase power is your organization's connection to the community you both share. Knowing their stakeholders had these options at their disposal, my client understood the benefit of getting ahead of the story first, guaranteed to be negatively received, but to attempt to mitigate the negative impact.

From experience working with clients and data curated from customer surveys, people prefer to buy their goods and services from companies that stand for a shared purpose or reflect their personal values and beliefs. Related, another report commissioned by Deloitte found top issues researched by consumers that influence their purchases include how the company treats its employees, treats the environment, and how it supports its community.[1] And across genders and generations a Nielsen survey uncovered respondents who said it is extremely or very important that companies implement programs to improve the environment.[2] Your community commitment is most effectively communicated with storytelling. And no, you don't need the storytelling resources of a video production unit, like the airlines, to tell your community story. A social media post, a webpage story, or blog will work just as long as the story is easily accessible and visible in relation to your product or service. For example, on your company's website, post your community story or a visible link to it. Whether your customer reads or engages with the content, they'll at least know the evidence of a community connection is there.

Furthermore, if your business relies on corporate sponsors or partnerships, they're looking for your community content to align with their community investment endeavours and may choose to reach out to you based on what they see or don't see. In fact, executives in charge of investing budgets for advertising campaigns want to partner with like-minded companies that have a great story to tell, especially in the community, so they can share that story like it's their own.

Sales and revenue

Whether your business makes up a product, service, or both, the bottom line is that you have to generate or obtain revenue to simply stay operational. Utility and quality, among other attributes, are important for the long-term success of your business, especially for developing relationships with repeat customers. Starting that relationship has to begin with some offer, enticement, or initiative, and for many companies that initiative starts with a story. Restating, your customers have choices, and all things being equal, the company that tells the better story, or even simply tells a story, ultimately wins their business.

Influence

Storytelling for business, like any other business strategy has objectives, and typically in order to achieve them, someone or some stakeholder group needs to be influenced to do something, change an opinion, or purchase your product. For example, the objective shared in this chapter's case study was to produce and distribute a story about a controversial policy announcement with the objective to influence key stakeholders first before the media did. Chapter 7, "Audience analysis", goes into greater detail about what audiences are influenced by your storytelling and what platforms you need to invest in to reach them. For example, if you want to influence government, primarily leverage the media as your platform to tell your story.

Selling success

Nothing sells and tells a story quite like the story of success. If your customers are benefiting from your products, services, or information, share the stories of how your customers' lives have become better as a result of your business. When working in the agriculture industry, we'd profile producers who used certain products from my clients that yielded greater results or how the products solved a longstanding and time-consuming problem. New customers who could relate were "sold" because they saw themselves in their peers and wanted the same results.

Online entrepreneur Stu McLaren has built an impressive online business that teaches entrepreneurs how to build their own membership sites by helping people transform what they know and love into recurring revenue. At the core of what McLaren markets is impactful and meaningful storytelling by consistently and relentlessly showcasing the success of his clients. For example, in his marketing emails, he'll copy and paste social media posts from his customers who sing his company's praises. Additionally, he'll interview successful clients who've done well by his programs. In a recent webinar, McLaren said this about the power of storytelling: "The stories of people experiencing your progress in your business are the most powerful marketing asset you can have – hands down."[3] Jeff Walker, who pioneered the way millions of people sell their products and services online with his Product Launch Formula extols the value of storytelling in his bestselling book *Launch*, stating "if you want to make your business and marketing memorable, then your marketing needs to tell a story".[4]

Business continuity (now and in the future)

If storytelling for business supports the growth of your business with new and repeat customers, business continuity is what will keep them coming back. Internally, consistent storytelling keeps your employees engaged with company narratives and cultural showcases. Even on a more functional level, for example, training videos for employees require a narrative (a "why"), and with it, you strengthen your engagement, which in turn keeps the business running behind the scenes.

Grow your story organically

No matter where you are on the storytelling continuum, the buy-in you get, literally and figuratively, will often come from how organically your stories are developed and delivered. As I'll remind you often throughout *Storytelling for Business,* you can't fake authenticity, and that's underscored with storytelling. Your stakeholders, many that know your business as well as or better than you do, can spot manufactured or disingenuous stories or even the elements (discussed in Chapter 2) within your stories. If you're going to invest in telling your story, keep it real, showcasing a problem or opportunity that really exists, and where possible, including the real stakeholders involved. Staying authentic was crucial to the case study's story. Even though the policy was controversial, the bigger problem was doing nothing at all to protect customers, with the only responsible solution being to introduce the new company mandate. Additional messaging showed similar policies were enacted in other jurisdictions with results that produced greater security for all involved.

Truth, transparency, and trust

Tell the truth, be transparent, and your business will be trustworthy. I'm not suggesting you have to open your financial records to the media, but consider opening more on the personal side of your business. Admittedly, there is a fair bit of risk with admitting vulnerability, and if you're in crisis mode (Chapter 8, "When a story goes sideways"), that will become even harder to consider. If you attempt any level of subterfuge in your storytelling for your business, you will run a greater risk of having your story exposed as inaccurate or embellished to make an exaggerated point or deflect away from an inconvenient problem you may be working through. Truth, transparency, and trust also matter when you're telling a success story for your business; however, state your intentions, even as a call to action, so your customers understand why they're investing their time to consume your content, otherwise, you run the risk of exploiting the goodwill of your content, and in the process, losing trust.

Narrowing your narrative

Depending on the size and scope of your business, you may have more options and storytellers at your disposal to tell your story. Resist the urge to include multiple messages and meanings within your story. Remember this chapter's opening case study's key message was keeping people secure, and any additional messaging was to support that overarching narrative. As you'll read in the next chapter, choosing a story structure can certainly guide you in keeping the story of your business focused. For example, if the objective of your story is to solve a problem, closely examine if you really need to get into explaining the symptoms of that problem as that may make the solution harder to understand. If your customers have found the story about why you're trying to solve a problem, it's because they're most likely currently experiencing the symptom, and don't necessarily need to revisit their frustration. Narrow your narrative, set the scene, and solve the problem simply.

When to tell your story (and when not to)

I once worked with an organization that would tell its story when tragedy struck someone in the community, in most cases, fatally. You might think it's insensitive to do so during such grief, but for this organization, its primary reason for existing is to prevent additional tragedies and further grief. And as hard as it is to engage stakeholders during such a difficult time, it's also the most opportune time to tell stories that emphasize prevention as people, normally distracted with so much other "noise", are listening and watching intently with others in their community. Again, be transparent and truthful in your storytelling intentions, and your stakeholders will understand why you're inserting your organization into the public discourse of a sensitive subject.

During the COVID-19 pandemic, not only did some companies choose not to produce any stories about their businesses, many shut down their operations completely as it was the right thing to do at the time to stop the spread of the virus in their communities. However, some remained "tone deaf" to the circumstances. By way of example, I remember one sport and leisure company located in a community hit hard by COVID, including significant deaths, producing content about how their products would be an ideal distraction. As you can imagine, the insensitivity of "enjoying" leisure equipment while others were fighting for their lives, was not well received. No one could fault this business for trying to survive during tough times, but the timing of telling their story could have been better, saving their stories of customers experiencing relief for when the threat of COVID wasn't as severe.

A cautionary tale

While some businesses use storytelling to successfully influence and sell, many organizations become a thriving operation because of a story. However, while an impactful narrative can build a powerful institution, it can also tear it down. For the

Canadian-based charity Free the Children, the power of story led almost every aspect of their brand, creating substantial donations (sales) and engagement with their brand, including years of sold-out arena tours led by their founders Craig and Marc Kielburger.[5]

The story goes that when he was 12, Craig came across the story of another 12-year-old boy, a child labourer, who was murdered after speaking up for children's rights. Profoundly moved by how a boy, like him, could be brutally slain for simply speaking out, Craig and his older brother Marc modestly launched their mission to free children and their families from poverty and exploitation, starting at their school.[6] From there, well, the rest is history, galvanizing the spirit of youth into a juggernaut of a charity and supporting tour called WE Day. If you've even been, as I have with my daughters, it's an aural and visual assault on the senses, all powerfully driven by stories from how WE Charity has made meaningful change in some of the most remote and poverty-stricken communities around the world. As we've covered, corporate sponsors want to align themselves with organizations and businesses that have good stories to tell, and WE Day, with a mobilized youth army, had countless community stories to tell. Reaching younger demographics is elusive, but highly desirable for sponsors, and WE Day provided a direct platform live in front of thousands of youth (by invite only!) in arenas and/or online.

With some irony, while it was the power of story that created the ethos by which WE Charity and WE Day thrived, it was this same storytelling power that decimated its reputation when a scandal tied to the governing party in Canada forced the charity to close its operations in that country. Remember this story's structure as we review a number of them in Chapter 2. I think WE Charity is on something of a hero's journey, currently going through a difficult time, though I hardly think we've read the last chapter on this enormously effective storytelling organization. Time will tell, and depending on when you read *Storytelling for Business*, we'll see if they did, in fact, return a hero.

Stakeholder benefit

If your stakeholders support and champion your business, your business will continue to grow and prosper. Making an outstanding product and offering a superior service are what will keep you in business, but first your customers, employees, and other stakeholders first must come to understand what you do. Furthermore, your audiences increasingly must understand what you stand for as a company. Storytelling for your business creates one of the most compelling and efficient strategies to reach as many stakeholders as possible at a time.

Intangible benefit

The challenge many business communicators still face is not all storytelling can be easily measured, but that outlook has changed dramatically thanks to the availability of data produced online, which we'll cover in greater detail in Chapter 10, "Making measurement matter". However, sometimes an experience, captured through the most convincing storytelling elements, can't be measured through the metrics we'll cover in Chapter 10. But well-produced stories compound engagement (internally and externally) over the long run, creating a sustained connection to your business. And where formal measurement is not available, the grapevine will do the job. My experience over the past 25 years, working and consulting for a wide range of businesses is that if your storytelling is working, you will hear about it from your customers, even anecdotally. Conversely, if your storytelling is not working, you're also going to hear about it, and it's typically expressed with greater emphasis from your stakeholders because they're invested in what you do. That, in it of itself, is another example of storytelling for business ROI.

Worth repeating

Case study: Storytelling for controversial content

- Use storytelling to communicate controversial content
- Make content accessible to the media, allowing them to embed your content into their content
- Build your storytelling around key messages
- Create your storytelling content in a way that can be repurposed across your channels of communication
- Understand that what content you share externally is also consumed by your external stakeholders

Storytelling at the boardroom table

- Increase in storytelling investment because leaders see that it works
- Use of storytelling language has become commonplace

The need to tell stories in business

- Remember my observation that business storytelling exists on a continuum that starts with the *onset* of a story leading across to a (desirable) *outcome*, and then back again, and so it goes
- Culture (internal and external)
- Community
- Sales and revenue
- Influence
- Selling success
- Business continuity

Grow your story organically

- Don't fake authenticity
- Present the genuine problem and the solution you're communicating

Truth, transparency, and trust

- Tell the truth and offer transparency
- Embrace the power of vulnerability

Narrowing your narrative

- Resist the temptation to include more messaging than necessary
- Narrow your narrative, set the scene, and solve a problem

When to tell your story (and when not to)

- Understand that sometimes the best time may be at the most sensitive time
- Contrast sensitivity with reality

A cautionary tale

- Recognize telling too much, too often can lead to scrutiny
- See how powerful storytelling created influential organizations like WE Charity, but also facilitated its downfall

Stakeholder benefit

- The people that matter the most to your business must understand what you do, along with what you stand for as an organization

Intangible benefit

- Embrace measurement of storytelling, but recognize even if you don't, feedback will make its way to you, both positive and negative

2

The story behind
the story

Case study: Call in the storyteller

For years, a city councillor in a small town where I was a reporter early on in my journalism career had tried just about everything to get a large corporation to clean up a neglected and problematic field of grass and tall weeds in his constituency. Over time, it became a dumping ground for garbage and location of illicit activity. On many occasions, neighbours shared stories of kids going in and coming out, and used needles strewn about the field. The councillor tried everything to get the large company to clean it up – no response. The last thing he wanted to do was cause any unnecessary harm to the company's reputation through the media, but kids were at risk, and feeling he had no choice, decided to call a local reporter he had met at various community events. After receiving the blessing from my editor, I took the story on. As a news videographer,

I captured the video of the blight of a field, spoke to neighbours, including one kid who had been pricked by a needle, and the story was broadcast later that day. The next day, large heavy machinery was on the site, cutting the weeds, and turning up and cleaning the soil. A fence went up with a notice about future development in the months ahead. After three years of asking the company to take responsibility, with no response, they finally took immediate action because of the negative publicity. The strategy: apply public pressure, via the media, to get the company to clean up its act. The tactic: leverage the media's reach and influence to tell the story. We'll get more into managing the media in Chapter 5 as just one of many tactics for telling a story to achieve an objective.

A look ahead

In Chapter 2, we provide a closer look at the story behind telling stories. The chapter explores what makes a compelling narrative for your business, including the structures, tools, strategies, and the science behind why people are influenced by the power of storytelling as evidenced by the opening case study, where the councillor leveraged the negative impact on people to influence the media to cover the longstanding challenge of getting a negligent business to take action. Building on the case study, Chapter 2 will provide you a fulsome perspective on what makes an effective business narrative, including storytelling structures, the elements to incorporate to bring the story to life, along with the essential resources you'll need.

The science of storytelling

We've all heard the saying "everyone loves a good story", including the councillor mentioned in the case study. Have you ever wondered why? To begin with, it sure does make us feel good or invokes emotions to provide a connection to the storyteller telling the story and what they're communicating. Getting the public concerned and to apply some public pressure on the company is why the councillor leveraged the media to tell his story, which it did, leading to a follow-up story that created a "happy" outcome – one of the most positive emotions for storytellers. Some argue there's more science to telling a good story than one might imagine. Dr. Paul J. Zak shared some of the outcomes of his research in the *Harvard Business Review*.[1] He wondered if he could motivate people to engage in cooperative behaviours by "hacking" the oxytocin system – all through the power of storytelling. Oxytocin is the hormone released into the bloodstream, usually in response to love or positive sentiment that is experienced. Accordingly, some call it the "love hormone". Rather than using face-to-face interactions, Zak used video stories. By taking blood samples before and after showing a character-driven video story, he found the body consistently produced oxytocin. Furthermore, Zak and his team assert there is a correlation between the amount of oxytocin in the brain and how much people were willing to assist others.

From blood to brain, the power of a good story for business also means people will have similar feelings derived from the narrative, facilitating that the message and sentiment from your story will be remembered. A story that is memorable is a win, especially in an age where so much external noise makes it extremely difficult to produce a truly memorable story, but when it works, it "clicks" according to neuroscience professor, Uri Hasson. He calls it "neural coupling" where responses in the brain "click" together when the brain determines a story is effective by whomever is sharing the story.[2]

Armed with this science, you can see how understanding the power of storytelling will be very good for your business, and it seems by example, so do many other organizations like charities, which often use feel-good stories to tug at your heart strings and your wallets or reinforce the success of campaigns that relied on your donations. Driving home the case study, the story presented a problem and the company (finally) provided the solution, with the media serving as the channel of communication to amplify the story.

What makes a good story for business

From the conceptual stage to the final editing stage, collectively I have always been guided by two groups of *essential elements*: internal and external. Internal consists of elements you have to rely on internally to make a compelling story for your business, such as emotions and critical thinking. External captures elements you rely on externally, such as people and places.

Internal elements

In greater detail, some of the *internal elements* that worked (most of the time) for me include:

Create a clear path

Your customers' time is valuable. If they open up your link online to consume your story, you better do your very best to make it worth their while, or you'll risk losing their trust and – just as importantly – their attention.

Solve a problem

Whether your business is a product or service or both, at times, your top task as a business communicator is to solve a problem for your customer. Don't be afraid to address the problem or challenge, leaning into it with simple solutions and delivered on the right channel (more in Chapter 4, "Choose your channel"). Your story should always answer questions, not create more.

Know your why and articulate it

When it comes to maximizing the power of storytelling, one of the modern-day masters is Simon Sinek and his book *Start with Why*. Sinek's comprehensive research asserts people won't truly buy into a product, service, movement, or idea until they understand the *why* behind it.[3] The councillor in the chapter's case study knew that as well, which is why he carefully formulated his "why" (get the land cleaned up once and for all) before reaching out to the media, as he would have risked ridicule from his constituents if he'd got it wrong.

Provide value

As a business storyteller, it's important to always ask yourself "after consuming the content I've produced, are my customers any better off for the experience?" In the case study, clearly, the community is better off with the field clean, opposed to having it littered with dangers that have hurt kids. Has your story provided value?

You can't fake authenticity

One of my all-time favourite mantras when it comes to storytelling for business across any medium with any message is you can't fake authenticity. From concept to execution, how authentic does every aspect of the story come across to your customers? Being consistently mindful of authenticity in business storytelling will guide you to staying true to your "why" and mitigates any intentional or unintentional use of elements that can be perceived as unauthentic. For the councillor, his aim was true: genuine concern to rid the neighbourhood of a danger that continued to threaten the well-being of the people who lived there.

Present conflict

Underpinning many compelling stories is conflict. That's exactly what this chapter's case study demonstrates: presenting the conflict of an unresponsive landowner whose negligence is leading to kids in the neighbourhood getting hurt. Depending on your perspective, or perhaps your mood right now, how you view conflict will change, but as a storyteller for your business, it's important to recognize any negative connotation with the word conflict because it's not always negative, it's also an opportunity to present a solution for your customers. For the councillor, the opportunity was to apply pressure to the landowner to clean up the property once and for all. Conflict doesn't always mean a dispute or something unresolved by one or more parties, it can also represent an internal conflict. Before you produce your story for your business, carefully explore the challenges your business faces, and how you can tell the story, allowing your customers to see themselves successfully engaging with your product or service or taking a desired action.

Prepare to be personal (vulnerable)

Whether you are proactively telling a heartwarming story about how your business brought communities together or fighting to keep your head above the turbulent waters of a crisis, prepare to be personal, even vulnerable in the tone of your story and those who are your main characters (see Chapter 6, "People power"). Customers who consume your stories, through any medium (aural or visual), will respond more favourably to your messages if they can connect to your business on a personal level.

External elements

With your internal elements identified, you can now begin to align them with the *external elements* to bring your story for your business to life.

Offer a call to action

This is *Storytelling for Business* after all, and you want to maximize value as noted above, so when appropriate, include a call to action within your storytelling to drive people to do something. This can include directing people to a company webpage or offering a promo code or discount, for example. However, remembering you can't fool your customer, be mindful not to waste their time or not provide value in your storytelling. If I think about my own content consumption habits, I will gladly subscribe to a newsletter (full of storytelling content) or YouTube channel if it provides me meaningful and worthwhile content that makes my life better in some way, providing value. In exchange, I offer the business storyteller something of even greater value – my time and attention. When creating and distributing your stories for business, treat your customers as you would like to be treated.

Call your own number

As you develop your story for business, selecting the optimal storyteller or spokesperson can include many people, most important of which is you! *Storytelling for Business* goes into greater detail in Chapter 6, "People power", but it is certainly worth the prelude here. The people you choose to tell the story of your business is one of the most important decisions you will make. For the councillor in the case study, while his self-interest may be to get re-elected, he saw the greatest value in being the lead storyteller to get the land dealt with.

Choose the right medium

Sometimes it's not what you say, but how and where you choose to say it, and that's particularly pertinent when maximizing the impact of the story of your business. The councillor could have chosen to share his plight in his weekly newsletter to constituents, but for maximum and immediate impact, he knew the mainstream media's reach would be his best option, especially as nothing else he had tried was working. I'll go in into greater detail on choosing the right channels for your story in Chapter 4, "Choose your channel".

Get it write

Early along my communications and content journey, a cherished mentor once told me that if you can write (creatively), you will never starve. That's not to take away from the many masterful technical writers out there, and believe me, that's an art in its own right, and perhaps a book for the future, but for now, as demonstrated above, the power to communicate at the some of the most impactful levels comes with telling a story – and that almost always starts with writing. Whether it's a script, a storyboard, an outline, or whatever tool you use to tell a story, you're going to need to write it down. And once you do, you'll then want to determine what tone, message, and direction you want your viewer or reader to take away.

What words work

When you have your stakeholder's attention, you will not have it for long, in fact just eight seconds according to research shared in a Microsoft report that analyzed attention spans.[4] I think you get the point – get to the point, and one of the most efficient methods of doing so is with your choice of words. Avoid jargon – you know your company's language, but don't assume that everyone else does. Cut out any unclear terms, unnecessarily big words, and acronyms. Speaking of acronyms, a simple, often used one is KISS (Keep It Simple Stupid). I think it speaks for itself. Back to big words, it goes beyond just the meaning, but the structure. Monosyllabic words (one syllable) are easier to remember than words with multiple syllables (polysyllabic). With some noted irony, the word monosyllabic isn't lost on me: one big word to describe words with just one syllable. Say something simple; three words, all starting with "s" to emphasize one meaning. This is alliteration. It can be effective to grab your customer's attention, but do so sparingly or strategically in your story or you risk losing the desired effect.

What to say and how to say it

Choosing strong active verbs provides clarity and direction for those who take in your content. Where the opportunity exists, avoid writing in the past tense or opting for the passive voice (for example: *Storytelling for Business* was written by Rob). Much better to use an active voice with an active verb (such as "wrote": Rob wrote *Storytelling for Business*).

To "be" or not to "be"

Elaborating on the previous section, when it comes to the passive voice (and whether to use or avoid), the verb "to be" comes in the form of eight words: be, am, is, are, was, were, being, been. As mentioned, the active voice makes your content easier to understand, but depending on your writing or storytelling style, using some passive voice *is* acceptable, providing some balance between the flow of information and style.

Not big on big words, jargon, or acronyms

Bigger is not necessarily better when it comes to the words you use when telling your story. When drafting your messages and content for your story, select shorter words (fewer syllables), making it easier for your audience to understand, and for your spokespeople to remember. However, if you need to say photosynthesis, say or write "photosynthesis" as that is the word to define the multiple stages by which plants use light to grow. Also, knowing your audience will guide your selection of words. If botanists make up your audience, you may risk insulting them if you choose not to use bigger words. Ultimately, researching and selecting the appropriate platform or medium before you begin to produce the story of your business will serve you well.

The same rationale applies for the use of jargon, keeping in mind your audience. Jargon refers to words or phrases that are unique to your business or industry. When communicating externally, I made a point of running my messaging by a few key trusted external contacts (outside the industry) to make sure they understood what I had written.

Less is more

Shorter sentences with simpler words make information easier to retain and recall. Another technique masterful storytellers rely on includes play on words, such as memorable phrases. For example, I could say "remember to use a short sentence with shorter words to attract paying customers" or I could say "the phrase that pays". Which is easier to remember?

Analogies and metaphors

Also known as a figure of speech, a metaphor uses an object or action to assist your customer as they visualize or comprehend your message. "Don't get shut out! Buy now before it's too late." In this phrase, "shut out" is the action, meaning you better purchase now before others do. An analogy compares one thing to another to aid in the explanation. For example, I was so busy today dealing with a whirlwind of meetings. Metaphors and analogies are extremely effective in explaining or simplifying what your story is trying to communicate, especially if the messages are new, abstract, or complex. By referencing what may be familiar to your customers or audience, you will make it easier for them to follow along what business is sharing in the story.

Get the message

From the perspective of telling the story of your business, when developing your messages, get crystal clear on what you are trying to achieve with your story. Knowing your company's business objectives streamlines the process of developing your messages.

Chart your storytelling course

Visuals

From day one of a ten-year career in television journalism, it was drilled into me (metaphor) that the best stories always start by writing to your best pictures. As you develop your story for your business, you will almost always have a more compelling and engaging story if you have the images and video to back up or illustrate what you are trying to communicate, sell, or influence. A helpful tip before beginning any storytelling project that requires visuals is to scan all the content; sometimes this can involve hours of video or gigabytes of images, hence the use of the word *scan*. You will quickly find that, at a glance, you will see your best content pop out. Write it down or shot list it by documenting where you saw it in your files. When you begin to draft your storyboard, instead of wasting valuable time trying to remember what could go where, you have already created a shot list, making it easier to reference your best pictures and video.

Storyboard

A storyboard, depending on your format, is essentially an outline for how your story will look and sound before it is produced. Some storytellers like to use online tools to document their best pictures and essential elements in a story arc or story structure, which will be covered later in this chapter. Others prefer the tactile approach of sketching rough images in boxes that give you a glimpse of what your story for your business will look like. The biggest advantage to using a storyboard is that it will save you a considerable amount of time if you need to revisit and will serve as your blueprint (analogy) as you build your story from start to finish.

Audio

Whether you tell the story of your business by podcast or video or other medium that benefits from sound, audio is an essential storytelling element, and one that gets often overlooked or underutilized. Audio creates suspense, excitement, and sets the mood, especially if your story is only using audio. In that case, audio truly puts your customer in a scene or environment where they are showcasing their visuals, complemented by voice, words, sound effects, and natural sound. The latter refers to the audio you capture as part of your storytelling production. For example, if your story's objective is to get your customers to attend a live auction, then the auctioneer's colourful calls will be a prominent element of the story, but do not forget to utilize the other audio like the audience response to the auctioneer as part of your story. The aural elements help your customer mentally interact with your product, service, or message by putting them there at the scene, complemented further by strong visuals.

Get in gear

An entire book could be written detailing the equipment needed for business storytelling. For focus and efficiency, I'm not going to delve into what equipment for what medium you should consider as the options would be almost endless and subjective to the end user's preference. Consider following my BEET (Budget, Equipment, Expertise, and Time) criteria. Hopefully, over time, you will find such an assessment can't be BEET. That play on words, by the way, is a pun, which – used sparingly – can help your customer remember an element of your story, in this case, my BEET acronym.

If you are exploring to tell your story in a significant way, use the BEET assessment to determine if your project needs to be in-house or out-of-house. In non-industry language, that means either doing it yourself (in-house) or hiring a professional (out-of-house).

Budget

Depending on the scope of the story you want to tell for your business, budget will ultimately be your guide on whether you go in-house (do it yourself, DIY) or out-of-house. For example, if you want a short one-minute video where you can simply do a show and tell in one take using your smartphone, perhaps you DIY, complemented with some simple lighting so both you and your product look good. If you want a slick, multi-camera shoot and editing effects, then you may want to consider going out-of-house if your budget allows. Budget can also be predicated on equipment and expertise, and the time it takes to accumulate both.

Equipment

Do you have the equipment you need to produce your story for your business, or do you need to hire someone who has already invested the considerable amount of time to research and money to purchase the gear? If telling your story is simple for something like a podcast where just a USB mic is required, then you may want to consider making the spend. However, if you want your podcast to have a high production value like studio quality sound, complemented by produced sound effects and introductions, then out-of-house may be your best bet. Before you make the final decision, spend some time investing in research. Some of the online tools and apps make it easier than ever to tell your story for your business.

Expertise

Expertise is often the deal-breaker between taking on a storytelling project yourself or with your content team, hiring someone else to do it, or deciding to hold off altogether if neither are an option. You or your team may have the budget and equipment, and the interest, but developing the expertise to conceptualize, produce, and distribute your story make take you considerably more time than you realize.

Again, the scope of any story you tell for your business comes to the level of production (if any) you require. For example, if you want to simply do a few videos for your vlog every month, then purchasing some basic lighting, microphone, and camera will suffice. When it comes to investing in creating personal expertise take the stress test: how stressed will you be investing the time into learning the tools and technology to tell your story? After you do your research, of course. If you feel stressed just thinking about it, hire someone in proportion to your project. If you feel buoyant and intrigued by keeping it in-house, now may be the time to give it a shot. For the out-of-house option, even if you have a content team, the advantages to working with an external team from time to time is that it will give you a new perspective on an old story or brand.

Time

If you have the time and genuine interest to research, or perhaps you have a keen communicator on your team that wants to add more content to your social channels, learning the basic equipment you need to tell your story, then consider doing it yourself (DIY) or keeping it in-house. That also includes the software and platform tools to create, edit, and distribute your story. If you feel time is better spent on your core competencies, after spending many hours trying DIY unsuccessfully, then going out-of-house will be the better option. Time is the variable most of the organizations I've worked with assess heavily when they choose to go out-of-house to produce some of their more sophisticated content pieces. And they're not alone, the Content Marketing Institute's 2020 study found that content creation is the activity B2B marketers chose to outsource regardless of company size, budget, and overall marketing success.[5]

Story structures

At its core, a good story structure consists of a beginning, a middle, and an end. However, sometimes which route you take along your storytelling journey depends on what story structure you choose for your business. It's fair to say, there are many models that are as old as the tradition of storytelling itself. I'll start with two structures that I have found particularly useful as a storyteller in business.

Pentadic Analysis

The first is the Pentadic Analysis developed by the often-cited rhetorician Kenneth Burke. He used a pentad consisting of five key elements to create a greater understanding of a story structure: scene, agent, act, agency, and purpose.[6]

> Scene: Where something in the story took place
> Agent: Who in the story did something
> Act: What in the story they did
> Agency: How in the story it was done
> Purpose: Why in the story it was done

Where many storytellers in business, particularly those in public relations, use the Pentadic Analysis to their benefit is shifting the story weight of each element within the pentad to influence the people that matter the most to take a specific action.

Freytag's Pyramid

If five is not your speed, then let's shift gears to seven with Gustav Freytag's Pyramid. The German playwright devised the structure to illustrate seven salient elements of drama within a story.

> Exposition: scene setting for the story
>
> Inciting incident: something begins, usually with something noteworthy
>
> Rising action: elements of the story are added or enhanced to build the story
>
> Climax: A part of the story that builds to the highest point of intensity
>
> Falling action: What happens after the highest point of the story
>
> Resolution: A natural resolution to an event, including conflict
>
> Denouement: The final unraveling of a plot

In storytelling for business, think of Freytag's Pyramid much like a mind map or an outline for business communications tools like a speech or statement or a script for a video.

Other story structures

Freytag's Pyramid is one of the more commonly used storytelling tools for business and brands, but certainly not the only one. Below are a few other storytelling structures you may want to consider as you develop your story for your business, keeping in mind the essentials we discussed earlier. Ensure that you can utilize some or all of them in whichever story structure you choose to get the most effective story.

In medias res

In medias res is Latin for "into the middle of things". Look to Freytag's Pyramid and start your story right at the climax. Where you go from there is ultimately up to you, but don't forget to keep the suspense throughout the story. For your business story, does your product or service enter at the climax? If so, how can your story solve a problem?

Hero's journey

The hero's journey is that age-old story structure where the lead (protagonist) adventures on to some kind of experience where she meets neat people, has some conflict and setbacks along the way, only to return home better for it all.[7] Can you think of how your story for your business could take customers on the same eventful journey?

Petal structure

Think of a daisy and its pollen centre as the core of your story. Each petal that connects to the core is a separate but related connected story that explains the central concept. This storytelling technique takes your customer on journey telling one related story after another before returning to the centre.

Nested loops

This storytelling structure is more common than you think. Returning to Simon Sinek's *Start with Why*, he developed the Golden Circle where he "decoded" what makes some leaders so inspiring. They start with the *why* at the core, telling the *how*, and *what*. That is similar to the nested loop story structure where the most important story starts in the middle, layered by other stories around it to support and explain it.

End with a cliff hanger

When you think of your favourite streaming service and the shows you binge watch or consume the entire series in short order, what keeps you going from one episode to another, and another, and another? By design, the producers of that content end each episode with a suspenseful cliff hanger where you just must find out what happens next. As a result, if you're like me and millions of others, you watch just... one... more episode. As the story of your business ends up in a series of content pieces, consider a suspenseful or enticing ending or hook to draw your customer into the next piece of content, and another piece of content, and another.

Worth repeating

Case study: Call in the storyteller

- Leverage the media's reach and influence to tell the story
- Assess the risk of losing control of some or part of your narrative when working with the media

The science of storytelling

- Understand storytelling evokes emotions in the brain, especially happiness
- Recall the correlation that a good story for business will produce positive feelings in the brains of your audience

What makes a good story for business

- Internal essential elements (what you rely on internally to make a compelling story, including intellectual ideas)
  - Create a clear path
  - Solve a problem
  - Know your why and articulate it
  - Provide value
  - You can't fake authenticity
  - Present conflict
  - Prepare to be personal (vulnerable)

- External essential elements (what you rely on externally to tell stories, including people and places)
  - Offer a call to action
  - Call your own number
  - Choose the right medium

Get it write

- Use words that work as you have a very short time to make an impression
- Plan what to say and how you say it
- Avoid the use of passive voice most times, but not always
- Use jargon and big words sparingly and strategically
- Structure sentences shorter
- Include analogies and metaphors
- Develop messaging with clear objectives

Chart your storytelling course

- Produce content that supports your best visuals
- Use a storyboard to plot out your story before you produce it
- Remember to not underestimate how good, good audio can be

Get in gear

- Assess three criteria when deciding to purchase storytelling gear or hire someone who has it: your budget, your expertise, and your time

Story structures

- Pentadic Analysis
- Freytag's Pyramid
- In medias res
- Hero's journey
- Petal structure
- Nested loops
- End with a cliff hanger

3

Build your own
media network

Case study: Building your own media network

Tired, frustrated, and unimpressed with trying to work with his regional media to tell the story of his business, Sam, the president of a large, proud, and progressive rural family-owned company expanded operations and sales to record levels during the first decade of his tenure, largely through consistent public and community relations' efforts, augmented with paid advertising through the 1980s and early 1990s. However, times were changing, and quite dramatically for those traditional channels of communication and storytelling. A recession leading into the turn of the 1990s and the nascent stage of the internet was on the horizon, metaphorically speaking, like a very dark storm system that was coming the media's way; more on that outcome in Chapter 5, "Managing the media".

As the years passed, Sam was blessed with a team of marketing early adopters, who were enthusiastically open to building their own media network, which included the company's website, social media, online content (videos) for external audiences and e-newsletters, virtual and in-person staff/supplier events, like townhalls, for their internal audiences. As the mainstream media network was becoming a less impactful option, while at the same time, becoming adversarial – a common dynamic that exists today for many companies – they had little choice to go it alone on their own "network" to keep up the brand's positive reputation, both internally and externally, top of mind with the people that matter most. As technology became more accessible with equipment and software coming down in price, the company began to accumulate the basic videography equipment, crucial to capturing content and producing their own customer success stories. Soon the power of computers and software programs allowed Sam's company to produce more stories, more often, complemented by the internet's mindboggling expansion to include a variety of platforms, making it easier to distribute their stories online. While social media's effectiveness is undeniable, so too was the power of email and email lists, which allowed the company to share stories directly speaking to their customers. As an early adopter, the company was able to establish its own media network with social media channels with a robust number of followers, hiring storytellers (social media and content managers) to share the company's narrative, both externally and internally. Ironically, thanks to the company's substantive social media presence, the mainstream media often cover the stories or posts for "free", almost eliminating the reliance of the mainstream media, which many companies in many industries are employing more often as part of their core storytelling strategies.

For the record, I will always advise working with the media at some point as part of a complete storytelling strategy. Explored in greater detail in Chapter 5, "Managing the media", integrating your social media storytelling strategy with a mainstream channel of communication can lead to profoundly beneficial results, carefully developed, of course. With media, especially rural media, closing their doors due to crushing online competition, Sam's business needed to invest in its own storytelling and develop a balanced strategy of producing content in-house, augmented by an out-of-house budget to support larger storytelling for business projects. Substantial challenges still exist, and I'll get into the pros and cons in greater detail later on. However, businesses are now able to independently tell their stories, thanks to advancing technology and accessible resources; they now have the choice to become their own media network, so to speak – something that would once have been considered out of reach. The early days of relying *just* on the mainstream media exclusively to tell the story of your business are all but over.

A look ahead

In Chapter 3, we introduce you to the concept of building your own "media network". The phrase is a much simpler way of saying finding your right mix of social media and online platforms, along with other traditional tools and tactics, and leveraging the media, as needed, to amplify the story of your business, as demonstrated by the family business in the opening case study. Furthermore, Chapter 3 explains how to distribute your storytelling content, complemented by ideas and concepts on how to maximize storytelling for your business. The chapter cautions not to become overwhelmed by near-infinite options and how to decide what media ultimately is best for the story of your business.

Fail to plan, plan to fail

If you fail to plan, then plan to fail. We have all heard similar mantras or sayings about the immense value of planning, and when it comes to creating your own media network to tell and distribute the story of your business, never has planning been more pertinent. With the heavy proliferation of online platforms and easily accessible tools to create the content, the options will become mind-numbing, and a potential enormous time-suck trying to figure out where to start and where to end up. What storytelling resources your business invests in will overwhelmingly be determined by how your customers consume content, what content they like to consume, and when they prefer to consume it.

So, how do you build your own media network to tell the story of your business? First, you need a plan, and your plan needs strategies, and those strategies need tactics. The plan comes to life through research and measured by objectives, which can provide data and other key performance indicators (KPIs) to assess if you succeeded. For example, the objective of your storytelling strategy is to create a 20% increase in website traffic to a specific product webpage within 30 days, and entice 15% of all visitors to click a special promotional offer that connects customers with sales representatives or other call to action.

Your content *plan* is the macro-level view explaining the rationale for the time, money, and energy you are going to invest into telling stories of your business. Your *strategies* (the *what*) are within the plan. Your *objectives* (the *why*) explain why it is all necessary and how you'll measure if the plan was successful. Your *tactics* (the *how*) represent the micro-level view of your content plan and how it will execute your storytelling deliverables, some of which we identified in the chapter's opening case study. And, as you'll read throughout *Storytelling for Business*, create your storytelling objectives and goals in alignment and support of the overall goals and objectives of your business.

All throughout your content plan, through development to execution to measurement, you'll need to determine who your storytellers (spokespeople, customers, staff, etc.) will be and what messages you're counting on them to deliver. I'll get into greater detail in Chapter 6, "People power".

Revisit the company's core planning documents

When it comes to storytelling planning, I could devote an entire chapter to this important strategic process. However, I've opted instead to present a high-level overview, giving me space to get in more storytelling for business content. But crucial to any stage of telling the story of your business, and worth the reinforcement throughout this book is to consistently evaluate and measure your storytelling against your core planning documents, including a strategic plan or your vision, mission, and values, as they ultimately set your business, and your storytelling content, apart from your competitors. They also provide clarity on what elements to capture or edit when the time comes.

Commit to a content calendar

Depending on your company's greater storytelling plans, you may have the need or desire to have multiple plans throughout the year or plans spread out over a few years to support a longer-term and sustained effort. For many businesses that invest in telling their stories, they are aiming to build momentum and keep it going. When you think in terms of a full year or multiple years, delivering the content to support the plan can seem like a daunting task. But it does not have to be if you build a content calendar. The calendar can be a tactic within the plan or high-level to include multiple plans, set strategically to key dates and timeframes.

As we explored earlier, as the technology to produce stories advances, so do to the tools and platforms to document how and when to share your stories with online content calendars. To mitigate the risk of dating this book, I will purposely not share or endorse the few free / paid platforms that I have benefited from using over the years. Not to mention, content calendars are customizable depending on preferences, and your best bet is to go to your favourite search engine and simply type "content calendar".

Old school works too

Perhaps you are "old school" and online platforms do not work for you and you prefer the tried-and-true spreadsheet or word processing document to outline your storytelling plan and content calendar. No problem, if you have considered the components outlined earlier in this chapter. Whether you are online or old school, if planning or even preparing to plan is new to you, the time invested at the onset of your storytelling for business endeavours will save you time exponentially over the course of your campaigns as you and your teams will remain focused, eliminating wasted time and resources trying to figure out what your plans have already clearly articulated.

Learning the learning styles

If you think of your own media network as "transmitting" its "signals" or communications on a frequency, the planning you have invested in will guide you to what channels your customers are "tuning" in to, so to speak. For example, I once worked with a client in the agriculture industry who was adamant in creating a network of almost exclusively audio content. He knew his customers spent hours (and hours!) in their combines or in machinery and wanted to listen to his content and the stories of his business while they worked. For his storytelling for business network, he told stories with weekly podcasts and producing a series of e-books that were also accessible via online audio services. The point to emphasize here is he had many options at his fingertips to build his network, but his planning led him to primarily use audio content for his storytelling because that was the learning style his customers preferred.

Chart your content course

Now that you have a better understanding of how your customers will absorb your storytelling, let's explore some of the more common modalities to tell your story. The most common fall into a model I call the *Telling Triad*, which consists of written, aural, and visual elements.

Written storytelling

Most thoughts become things when they are transferred from your mind and documented on paper (or word processor or online app, whichever you choose), and in many cases, how you tell the story of your business will originate with writing, including blogs, articles, and webpage copy. For a deeper dive, some businesses write white papers or reports. We will take a closer look at the platforms and suggestion in Chapter 4, "Choose your channel". Also, how you develop the plan to tell your story also starts with writing. While you do not have to strive to be a published author, suffice it to say that storytelling for business will require you to write at some level as some point.

Aural storytelling

Going back to the example of my client in the agriculture industry who told stories using audio tools like podcasts, he also preferred to tell the stories of his business that way. When we developed his storytelling plan, he shared his insecurity of not ever being much of a storyteller. I knew otherwise. Generally quiet and shy, he is incredibly intelligent and well-spoken, and well-respected in his industry as a leader. He was passionate about his business's products and services, and no one knew them better. He was the voice of the brand and I encouraged him to purchase a small MP3 voice recorder or use the voice recorder on his smartphone to record his story ideas as they came up throughout the day. When it was time to turn his thoughts into things, he returned to his initial recordings, using them as outlines for podcasts, which he produced monthly. If you like to speak and best express the value of your business, choosing to tell the stories of your business may be best served aurally.

Visual storytelling

In our opening case study, during the planning phase of any storytelling campaign, the team asked the audience with surveys how best to deliver content, and based on feedback, consuming visual stories was indeed believing. This rationale and data would also explain why video is such a powerful medium. For example, if your story's objective is to show and tell how your product works, visual storytelling is the best route to take as visual learners like to see it in action for themselves.

Tactile storytelling

While not directly included in the Telling Triad, tactile experiences are very effective to complement your storytelling, utilized through the triad. This would explain why tradeshows are part of a multi-billion-dollar industry or why so many brands have taste booths in stores. Their storytelling efforts have brought their customers to their actual products, now a tactile storytelling experience where customers can touch, taste, feel, or generally experience the sensations that their stories were attempting to explain.

Too much, too soon

I have worked with companies, well-resourced with multiple content teams, and where they have succeeded most is by focusing on only what they needed to build their own storytelling network. The temptation is there to secure multiple social media handles, start a podcast, create a video content series, write weekly blogs, develop a complex website, and on it will go. But while your business is creating all that content, who is running your business and how is all that content being paid for if you are not doing it yourself?

One of my all-time favourite business thought leaders is Seth Godin. You might be surprised to learn he built his own media network almost exclusively using just one platform – blogging. In an online streaming workshop he shared the importance of why he picked blogging when he started in the late 1990s because he understood his audience would best consume his content through blogging. In more succinct terms that are hallmark to Godin, when it comes to telling your story, he counsels "pick your place".[1]

Content is king, but access is the kingmaker

In your research to build your own media network to tell the story of your business or organization you've probably read or heard the saying "content is king", which essentially means content is truly one of the best ways to tell the world about your product or service. "Content is king" is a saying many business storytellers have rightfully adopted, but I've added the qualifier "but access is the kingmaker". With most successful businesses that tell their story, they connect with their customers because they give them access they can't get elsewhere. Having worked in professional sports for a number of years, fans always shared they wanted more access to players and to get behind the scenes to see and experience a "day in the life" of a professional sports team. Now suffice it to say, your business doesn't have to be a professional sports team to provide access, and in your storytelling development process, dig deep to share some behind-the-scenes content on how your business does what it does. I'm not suggesting open your financials, but, for example, if you're in manufacturing, take your customers on a "never seen before" tour of the production facility, showcasing all your great employees in the places you're most of proud of that make up your business.

It's not what you say but how you say it

Let's say your intention for storytelling was to inform your customers about how your product or service solves a problem, but in the end you scare them away completely by focusing too much at the issue rather than the solution. This is just one scenario (of many) in which a storyteller can use elements (as discussed in Chapter 2) harshly or too vividly. The *tone* of your message is vividly reflected in the choice of words, imagery, and video you choose to tell your story. The same goes for your *style*. As part of your storytelling planning, give ample consideration to the style of how you want to tell your story. For example, do you want your style to be formal with more jargon and come across as more matter of fact or more casual with language that is simpler?

The purpose is to repurpose

If there is only a handful of theories or best practices you adopt from *Storytelling for Business* please let repurposing your content for storytelling be one of them. For example, if your own media network consists of a website, e-newsletter, podcast, and a few key social media channels, when you produce a story to share with your stakeholders, plan to repurpose one story for each platform. Let's say you decide to produce a video to explain how your new product works. Even before you begin, plot out how the content you create for that video story can be used (repurposed) again for your other channels of communication. Perhaps in your product story, you interview a service manager on camera to explain the benefits. From the video, you can transcribe the interview into written form as the basis for your blog or webpage article. The video clips can be reformatted into audio files that can serve as the focus of your next blog. Or the video itself: cut down the longer video into short bite-size video clips you can schedule out on your content calendar, leading up to the release of your longer video and the product launch itself. As part of your planning, which we reviewed earlier in this chapter, if you do decide to invest in a bunch of storytelling platforms then repurposing your content is one of the most effective storytelling strategies to make the process less burdensome. From maximization point of view, when you create a story for your business, the purpose is to repurpose.

Worth repeating

Case study: Building your own media network

- Evaluate your media landscape as part of the decision to build your own media network, as the team in the case study did
- Evaluate when to leverage the media as part of your own media network, remembering that some level of mainstream media inclusion is always worth considering
- Expect mainstream media coverage as you produce your own storytelling content, even if it's exclusive to your network

Fail to plan, plan to fail

- Review core components of storytelling and content planning include strategies (the what), your tactics (the how), your objectives (the why), along with key messages
- Review the company's core planning documents, including strategic plan, vision, mission, and values to provide clarity on what to include and not include
- Commit to an online content calendar to plan out your storytelling, and don't forget to include everyone who needs to be a part of the process

Old school works too

- Consider traditional platforms to plan your business storytelling if you eschew online tools. As long as you're writing your ideas down in one place that can be easily revisited and shared with others is what matters most.

Learning the learning styles

- Learn how your audiences want to consume your content – the majority may prefer listening or watching, by way of example

Chart your content course

- Explore three common modalities for storytelling: written, aural, visual – and for honourable mention, tactile storytelling

Too much, too soon

- Resist the temptation to take on more social media channels and other platform than you really need – remember Seth Godin's wise counsel, building his empire with blogs: "pick your place"

Content is king, but access is the kingmaker

- Give your audience exclusive access with the content you produce
- Consider behind-the-scenes storytelling to provide truly unique content people online crave

It's not what you say but how you say it

- Consider the tone of words you choose to communicate messages in your stories (jargon or simple language)
- Examine the style of how you want the story to be perceived (formal or informal)

The purpose is to repurpose

- Produce content once with the intention of using it in other media to amplify the story's reach (using audio from video for podcasts)

4

Choose your channel

Case study: Pivot or perish

Like so many business owners, Sara, a solopreneur who had a thriving speaking, training, and consultancy operation, had to pivot her business, or see it perish when the COVID-19 pandemic literally shut down her industry overnight in March 2020. Thankfully, and yet another reason to build your media network and invest in telling the story of your business, Sara had been a progressive and proactive storyteller on her social media and online channels of communications for the past decade. Additionally, through a concentrated effort, she had also amassed a considerable email list well into the thousands, which would serve her well as she need to communicate to her stakeholders that the next chapter in her story was going to be an extremely difficult one, as it was for many people, especially those who were self-employed.

While she was aware of virtual training platforms to offer training online, Sara had yet to embrace the opportunity as she quite enjoyed the travel and speaking/training groups of all sizes live and in-person. But that opportunity was not going to be available for the foreseeable future due to lockdowns and restrictions that shut down events and public gatherings, which ended up being many months more than anyone had anticipated.

As you might expect, given her background and the ability to pivot to leverage her own media network, Sara jumped in an embraced online training through a few key platforms. The benefit Sara had over many others who not only had to ramp up or start from scratch, she had invested years in narrowing down her channels of communication to just a select few, so when she had to add online training by video conferencing, she once again resisted the temptation to try to incorporate using more than one, instead choosing the platform that integrated well into her own media network (social media, email lists, websites, video content).

As pandemic restrictions eased, and Sara, along with other businesses, slowly eased back into the public assembly realm, her need for virtual platforms subsided, but not entirely. Even though society at-large was suffering a severe virtual fatigue, Sara still kept a component of her online presence available to her stakeholders, even though many of them preferred to connect with her live, as she wanted to mitigate the pain of pivoting again, even if it meant investing in a medium that wasn't as necessary as it once was during the lockdown pandemic months.

A look ahead

In Chapter 4, we take a deeper dive into why people consume content on social media, and by extension, the stories on your own media network. For Sara, in the case study, having her own media network wasn't just a "nice to have", it was a "need to have" during the pandemic, giving her an invaluable mechanism to keep connected with the people that matter the most to her business. Chapter 4 covers how to choose your channels, making your storytelling amenable to the people that matter the most to your business via these platforms (your own media network), plus how your business can benefit by including them in your business storytelling.

One or one too many

As illustrated in Sara's story, choosing the right channels of communication to tell the story of your business not only grows your business but can keep it operational in times of crisis or during unprecedented times, which the pandemic was tirelessly referenced as. In this chapter, we go into greater detail about the different mediums, but by design, unless it is a staple (Facebook, Google, etc.), I will not get brand specific to avoid dating this book because many platforms, especially on social media, come and go. At the same time, according to the Pew Center, its research found in 2021, that approximately 84% of American adults used at least one form of a social media platform, an almost meteoric rise from 5% in 2005 when researchers started tracking the use of social media in the US.[1]

Now that we have discussed planning in previous chapters, you now know what type of storytelling content you want to produce, and now you have to distribute it by choosing your channel or channels. I recommend starting with one or two anchor channels, becoming proficient and efficient, lending to a consistent and credible stream of business storytelling. Remember in Chapter 3 how Seth Godin built his enormous following online through primarily just one platform – blogging – but has now embraced video as part of his storytelling efforts. This strategy of "less is more", by example, allows your business not to spread itself too thin on content distribution. From here, explore other channels of communication, through repurposing, to complement your anchor channels. For example, if the story of your business is to showcase employee culture, use a professional, work-related social platform like LinkedIn to post your videos and web articles to. From there, you can expand this strategy by sharing the stories on your internal e-newsletter, intranet, and more.

Understanding social media

Before we start to take a closer look at some specific platforms to tell the story of your business, it is important to understand why your customers use and rely on social media. Social media is everywhere, accessible and convenient. In the hands of the majority of your customers are smartphones, linked to a network that streams content 24/7. In 2018, the population of Canada, where I live, was just over 37 million people.[2] And, in the same year, Statistics Canada estimates approximately 88% of Canadians were mobile subscribers.[3] Now just because that endless stream of content is accessible, it does not make it easier to tell the story of your business. In fact, it becomes more difficult if you do not know where to start, execute, and finish. Thankfully, you have *Storytelling for Business*. The point to emphasize here is you are in the storytelling game in a meaningful way thanks to social media; whereas before, it was only the mainstream media that predominantly was the gatekeeper of whether your business story was shared to a wider audience.

To stay connected

Humans are social creatures and at the core of the human condition is our need to belong to a group. Social media, for better or for worse, provides an immediate and easily accessible method to stay connected to people we feel are most important.

To be informed

As time goes on, increasingly more major social media platforms are agreeing to pay publishers of news for their editorial content. These platforms, many of which we use daily, are facing public pressure to pay for the news content they share because that is what many of their users are doing – sharing news editorial to be and stay informed. Social media users are also craving to stay informed with their tribes, whether it be updates on critical matters in their communities or banal stories on what they had for dinner.

To be entertained

In Canada, as in most industrialized countries, people are on their phone a lot. According to Statistics Canada, 56% of Canadians check their phones before they go to sleep, and while they're awake, 45% check their smartphones every 30 minutes,[4] though I expect those numbers will only grow with more time and with more research. For a variety of reasons outlined in this section, but most predominantly here, people spend time on social media to be entertained, and as a result, content producers have grown very large, very quickly, not to mention very profitable.

To get educated

During the COVID-19 pandemic, billions of people "locked down" to stop the spread of the deadly virus turned to the internet to use their new-found abundance of discretionary time to get educated.

Webinar platforms boomed because they facilitated the ability to connect large numbers of people to learn and engage, as we shared in the case study at the beginning of this chapter. Furthermore, businesses leveraged the extra eyeballs to tell their stories to remain in contact with their customers by educating them with their products and services. Even prior to the pandemic, people around the world invested billions of dollars into learning online.

To feel engaged

Where the story of your business has some of the most potential to make an impact is through engagement. Social media platforms make it easy for people to engage with your stories, providing instantaneous feedback and engagement mechanisms like "likes", re-posting, and comments. Analyzing engagement of similar businesses like yours also provides a valuable resource to research what may or may not work for telling the story of your business.

Go live

For many businesses wanting to tell their story, they are choosing to do so in real time – live. For Sara and her business, when she couldn't see them in-person during the pandemic, connecting to them live on social media via live video Q&A sessions, in her words, saved her business, and in many ways made it stronger as her customers appreciated and enjoyed the online interaction. A simple online search will net you a number of viable options that allow you to stream live from your phone or with a full studio on a broadcast quality stream. Having an immediate, direct connection to your audience is palatable for many businesses as it can display a greater sense of connectivity and two-way communication.

Going live does not come without risk. Not knowing the technical aspects of a webinar or social platform alone can crash your live storytelling just as much as it can elevate the experience. Moreover, when you are live, you are out there, and mistakes, even with no ill-intention, taken out of context can be amplified rapidly on social platforms, with little recourse until after the damage is done. Going live and engaging your customers online has many benefits, but it is an area where planning – a common theme throughout *Storytelling for Business* – is especially vital.

Janet Stewart, a leading Canadian online education expert once told me in her own webinar, that for every one hour of webinar training, plan to invest 71 hours in preparation.[5] When working in a live platform to connect with your customers, that may seem like more time than you are willing to invest but consider the greater cost of hosting hundreds of your customers live, only to stumble or suffer some form of catastrophic technical failure. The more you invest in time spent planning, the greater return you can have educating, influencing, or selling with your story.

If live does not jive with your business storytelling, that is fine. In fact, most businesses I have worked with do not engage in live storytelling for their businesses, or do so on a limited basis, choosing instead to go "live-to-tape" or produce "look live" stories in short- or long-form. An example of this may be instead of going live with a Q&A session about your new product, record it as if you are live, and then upload and distribute the recording after the session is produced. Going live-to-tape gives you the opportunity to try what it is like to go live, but correct any (big) mistakes, complemented with some production elements. Notice how I put "big" in brackets. If authenticity is important to your business storytelling, I encourage you to leave the small mistakes or stumbles in, as long as it is not a distraction, to show you are just like the rest of us – human. Remember: you can't fake authenticity and being real in your storytelling provides that opportunity.

Practice makes progress (not perfection)

Live webinars were new to Sara, and as nervous as she was to try live, she killed it on her first attempt all because she practised several times in advance, allowing her to get comfortable with the technical aspects and the performance of being live "on-air". Earlier I pointed out through research it takes dozens of hours or preparation for just one hour of live content. Even if you're relatively savvy with technology and online platforms, they have advanced considerably due to the overwhelming demand of the pandemic, throwing a lot of businesses into the live realm before they were ready. I'm sure you can recall your own experiences witnessing too many awkward live presentations where the host got flummoxed by platforms that did not perform as expected or challenges with the Wi-Fi that caused long or indefinite pauses, which you also need to plan for.

Once you've chosen your live platform and the tools to deliver your content, make the worthwhile investment to schedule in at least three sessions before you go out to your full media network.

- Practice session *live*, telling no one. If you don't want to use your branded social media channels, create a new one with an anonymous handle to get you started.
- Practice session *live* to a small group of invited peers you can trust to give you constructive feedback.
- Practice session *live* to a small group of your invited customers.

And, even before you step in front of a webcam or something higher quality to capture your image, practise how to use your gear, if you're going to go live on your own, and many do quite successfully, don't let your gear technically trip you up – it will if you don't learn how to use it well. Even the platforms you use have many tools and enhancements for you to utilize, but like anything else when presenting, learn them inside out, practising them thoroughly before you go live.

Note the heading for this section – "Practice makes progress (not perfection)". No one is ever perfect live on any medium, and that's what makes going live so attractive. If you can have a great performance, it shows your customers you're deeply committed to offering content to truly serve them. You will have setbacks and awkward moments live – absolutely everyone who presents live does at some point, and the true measure of a live storyteller is not only how well they do when things are going well, but how well they do when things don't. Even simply releasing the need for "perfection" and anticipation for live snafus can make all the difference, sharing with your audience that this is sometimes the reality of going live. As part of your planning, make sure to have back-up plans in place such as a toll-free conference call number in case you simply can't get back online in front of a camera and/ or a plan for alternative Wi-Fi if yours goes down. The objective here is not to scare you but to prepare you. When you pull off a live, virtual event for your customers, it's a tremendously gratifying experience as you've put yourself out there and you've connected directly with your customers, both current and new.

Go with graphics

When it comes to creating and producing the story of your business, going big is not always necessarily better, meaning you do not always need a large video production to get your message to your customers when a simpler treatment will do, like a graphic. For example, if your business needs to influence customers to do something, designing a series of graphics for your social media channels with short, snappy messaging and colourful, on-brand design elements can be sufficient to get people to view and engage with your story. Graphics also provide an opportunity to click through to your business website or to some other channel of communication that provides more information. I know my graphic designer contacts will cringe when I share this, but you can get some decent graphics designed online with do-it-yourself platforms or through online freelance bid services. However, like any product or service you choose, you sometimes do get what you pay for, and while working directly with a designer to create your graphics may cost you more, it can save you more time than trying to navigate cheaper options to get what you really want.

Email still excels

With the enormous growth of social media, many social media pundits expected the use of email would diminish in contrast. Think about your own communication habits and tools, especially at work. I am willing to bet you still share information with your colleagues or personal contacts predominately through email. For those who champion email, as I do, the reason it remains a dominant method to distribute the stories of your business, or even be the platform where your stories originate from, is that email not only evolved with social media, but has innovated along the way. After you give your name and email to sign up for updates and content from your favourite brands, what usually follows is a predetermined series of automated emails designed to get you to engage with the content. In your favourite search engine, type "email newsletter" and you will be presented with dozens of sophisticated email platforms that manage hundreds of thousands, even millions of contacts. For this reason, many business storytellers anchor their content directly (written stories, graphics, etc.) or indirectly (links to videos, webpage stories, etc.) into email newsletters, which is a strategy Sara employs quite successfully, and she learns a lot from the data the online newsletters produce, giving her great insight into what storytelling content is working and what is not. Each link or simply opening her newsletter itself tracks and then produces a wealth of engagement data via a backend platform, rich with a dashboard of data. I will get into the potency of email measurement in Chapter 10, "Making measurement matter". Most people hold their email inboxes as sacred space because they depend on them as their primary business communication tool, and if you can build trust with your customers, producing and sharing compelling storytelling content, they will let you in and let you stay there.

Get it white!

If your business needs to tell its story using a lot of data, theories, and complex messaging, a white paper will work as a valuable channel of communication. A white paper is a document, usually in PDF format, that is available for download (in exchange for your name and email) from a website or social post. Also known as background reports, content marketers have used the same principle to create white papers for businesses, rich with valuable insight and industry related data. Depending on the objectives you are trying to achieve with your white paper, it can vary in scope and quantity. I have found with most white papers, there is some tacit objective that weaves its way through the white paper to build trust with you as an authority, and from there, influence you to a call to action. That action can be to become an advocate, share the message, or reach out to purchase a company's product or service. Personally, I am a sucker for a "good" white paper, and I will give up my email and name to download it, and I will stay on that company's email list if it remains worth my time to consume interesting and informative content. If this seems like the *white* stuff for you, do a quick gut check before you dive in as you'll need to be prepared to invest time and energy into producing good quality documents, which includes a fair bit of research to back up your insights and data. I have read too many white papers that were light on insightful content or storytelling examples, and heavy on sales pitches. As a result, like most people, I immediately disengage, unsubscribe from the originating email list, and lose trust with that company.

When to post and share your story (not a one-size-fits-all)

Understanding how social media platforms perform best and determining when the best times are to post your stories for your business can be tricky, and in some cases, very complicated to understand if you want to dive into the complex world of social media algorithms that determine how these platforms work. But the good news is, you don't necessarily have to, as it is in the best interest of any social platform to share this information with you in the simplest terms. Additionally, there are social aggregator services where you can channel all your social platforms through that also provide the meaningful data and insight to support or critique your storytelling. What I have found most elucidating after analyzing various social platforms is optimal posting times do differ from one popular platform to another, and sometimes drastically. As part of your planning and content calendar development, it is important to know or have an idea of who your customers are as that will allow you to align that data with the data shared by social platforms on when best to post content. Don't forget to make scheduling content a core part of your overall content calendar. In addition to committing to a content storytelling calendar, Sara made it a core part of her business, scheduling in bi-weekly meetings with her supporting team to discuss story ideas, and when best to distribute them to the people that matter the most to her company.

Writing for social media

Every social media platform differentiates itself from others by a variety of guidelines. Some platforms only allow you a certain number of words or characters or restrict use of hyperlinks and video. Nothing some editing cannot mitigate, but no sense investing more time than necessary if you are only posting to social media over writing for a blog or a white paper. Additionally, social media platforms create their own style guides, made accessible for users to understand how to draft posts.

Best time to send email

If your business story is driven through email campaigns, much like social platforms, getting a better understanding of your email platform's metrics will serve your campaign better. However, while social platforms differ dramatically in use and function, email remains standard in its operation, whether for personal or professional use. According to some of the larger customer relationship management (CRM) services that manage email campaigns, in general, when people begin or end their day is the time they often have to check and catch-up on email, and they are doing so during the week, according to HubSpot. Its research indicates highest click-to-open rates are 10am, 1pm, and 6pm.[6] That said, do not discount weekends either as time where people avoid email, even as it relates to their work email accounts. On weekends, without the stressful distraction of work deadlines, and generally more discretionary time, your email campaigns can be revisited. I have found with a number of companies I have worked with that after sending out their email campaigns during the week in the "sweet spot" times noted above, which lead to desired open rates, the click-throughs to engage with their storytelling, they still received additional content engagement in the evenings or weekends. Like most rules, there are always exceptions; knowing your audience and their viewing preferences will help guide you.

Websites work!

No matter what type of storytelling platform for your business you choose, the primary objective of the content you have worked so hard to create is to do one thing: drive people to your website. In Sara's storytelling, her primary call-to-action is to visit her website for more information. Like Sara's business, your number one storytelling tool is your website. Using the appropriate metaphor, think of your website as a web with each strand of that web as your storytelling content, whether that be a social post, a white paper, or a video, all leading back to the centre – your website or a webpage. From a business storytelling perspective, your website is the place for all your content to live. If your own media network to tell your stories includes blog posts, videos, and social posts, they should all have a presence on your website. Many businesses that invest in storytelling for business archive their stories on separate "media" or "our story" webpages, allowing their customers to see, hear, read, and experience the full context of the business's storytelling. However, too much storytelling content has a way of getting away from many businesses. A worthwhile strategy of your storytelling plan to include is regular audits of the storytelling content that lives on your website; otherwise, you risk having stale or out-of-date content which can even counter your current storytelling initiatives. Furthermore, as your content is online, it has a digital footprint that is easily shared, and can be easily forgotten by a business that created it years ago.

As this is a book about storytelling for business, and not a website design book, I will not get too far into design, but the reason websites work so well with social media is all in the code. The major social media platforms where your business stories are often posted can be embedded into your website pages. By design, this facilitates greater cross-platform engagement, and allows you to let the social platforms show up-to-the minute updates. Most social platforms let you copy and paste your posts or even full streams directly into your website effortlessly. For Sara, the strategy of using embedded social streams on her website allowed her to repurpose her storytelling across numerous platforms, all at the same time.

Of course, websites have become so much more than just storytelling platforms, and as a result can consume a lot of your time and money, but the good news is you do not have to know how to code to create a solid website for your storytelling. Use your favourite search engine to find template-based websites, which have grown substantially because their ease-of-use and effectiveness to reach customers. These do-it-yourself (DIY) platforms allow you to get into the online storytelling game without breaking your budget, but they still will require your time and effort to keep your site and, more importantly, your content current. Many businesses that have become quite advanced in telling the stories of their business through their own media networks choose to work with web designers to manage their websites, giving them more time to create and share great stories. Whether you DIY or hire a web professional, both options have their benefits.

If storytelling for your business requires a large volume of content in a short amount of time and/or it is separate campaign altogether, many companies I have worked with have launched separate websites to host this level of storytelling. The advantages of investing in separate websites on separate domains include creating more emphasis on a specific storytelling campaign, reducing excessive content on your main website, and providing a direct channel of storytelling which can be linked to and away from.

Traditional still has traction

My introduction to mass communication out of school started with a behind-the-scenes job working in radio in the early 1990s. Even back then, media watchers predicted doom and gloom, and eventual end to traditional radio stations due to a recession and declining ad sales and interest. Furthermore, with competition from the internet, radio was predicted to dissolve into the ether like the very airwaves that carries its signals. Now, well into the 2020s, radio is still here, and some would say stronger than ever, but not without its challenges. The point here is that the traditional forms of media, which also include television and print, remain a viable option for leveraging your storytelling for business. A 2018 US Pew Research Center report shared that television, while declining steadily, still remains the most popular platform where Americans get their news.[7] As mentioned earlier, social media giants are investing in traditional news services, as that is where a large percentage of their users share content from, and why the next chapter has been devoted to working with the mainstream media.

It's all in the packaging

If you have ever purchased an Apple product, it is a fair bet that the packaging their products came in were as sleek and well-designed as the actual products themselves. Figuratively and literally, that is by design. Apple's packaging, in and of itself, tells a story for their business, which the company shares widely and proudly. In 2017, the company posted its own white paper, sharing in great detail its paper and packaging strategy.[8] Once again, the writing is as beautiful as the packaging it describes with well-crafted phrases that include strong adjectives and vivid active verbs, such as "source virgin fiber responsibly", "protect and create sustainable working forests", "sequestering carbon", and so on. If your business produces products, and you are looking to tell its story, the packaging or the environment in which it is used or experienced can play a part in your business storytelling strategy. For example, how many times have you seen marketers for major brands decal the stairs for a leading soft drink in your favourite concert hall or on the walls outside the venue? The packaging and environment are two mediums that are also tactile and experiential and can be further complemented with call-to-actions (CTAs) using specific webpage or websites as noted above, or QR codes and special inserts. The CTAs also produce some rich data that can assist in the measurement of success of your storytelling. More on that in Chapter 10, "Making measurement matter".

Let someone else tell your story

Working with other industries, partners, and external stakeholders can prove challenging, managing conflicting and competing self-interests, but if you can successfully align on a purpose, the reach and impact to tell your story (and theirs) can be exponentially greater.

Creating a strategic alliance has worked well with charitable and non-profit organizations I have worked with over the years. While they compete for the public's attention and donations, there are times where working together to tell a story about an issue will get more mainstream and social media attention than if each organization had tried to go it alone. My direct experience with creating and then managing strategic alliances to tell a story is that it usually takes one storyteller to lead the campaign's strategy and the development of tactics. The advantage to leading is you have the greatest influence, but you also have a greater workload managing the campaign and the competing self-interests. Worth the effort? Yes, but not all the time. I find investing an hour or two in an exploration meeting with your partner leads will quickly give you the insight you need to align strategically, go out along, or simply leave it altogether. And the latter can happen as the exploration meeting provides some insight from like-minded people and organizations that usually present some perspectives you may not have considered.

Leverage someone else's platform

In Sara's case, she looked around her industry to find other speakers and trainers who could complement her business and content, and if they had an established media network of their own, she collaborated with them to produce joint online live events like webinars and masterclasses, and in the process Sara's business got exposed to new audiences. Furthermore, she collected hundreds of new emails (potential customers!) as her colleagues agreed to share contacts and data from the event.

Worth repeating

Case study: Pivot or perish

- Invest in your own media network for when unforeseen circumstances (pandemic) shut your business and industry down

- Incorporate a mix of online and in-person offerings to your customers

One or one too many

- Start with one or two core social media channels, and add more (if necessary) from there

Understanding social media

- Understand the core reasons people use social media include:
  - To stay connected
  - To be informed
  - To be entertained
  - To get educated
  - To feel engaged

Go live

- Explore the benefits of connection with the people that matter the most live online
- Mitigate the risk, but forge ahead!
- Practise live online at least a few times before going out to public
- Embrace that live practices makes progress, and not perfection

Go with graphics

- Produce graphics for your social media channels as effective and simple way to tell your story
- Ensure to include call-to-action items, including visiting your website

Email still excels

- Learn to leverage that email remains one of your customers top online activities to consume your storytelling content

- Explore online email programs that repurpose your storytelling content and curate great data for measurement

Get it white!

- Consider white papers if you need to communicate concepts and ideas that require a great deal of information

When to post and share your story (not a one-size-fits-all)

- Get to know when the best times are to share your stories with the people who matter most
- Ask them what times/dates they prefer, using survey or even a simple email reach-out

Websites work!

- Remember your website is your #1 storytelling tool
- Showcase and archive your storytelling on your website
- Harvest rich and insightful website data from tools like Google Analytics

Traditional still has traction

- Remember to include traditional channels – it may be easy to overlook them with so many online options

It's all in the packaging

- Recall how Apple uses its packaging to tell a story? If you've ever unpackaged a new iPhone for the first time, you'll get it

Let someone else tell your story

- Create strategic alliances with other industries to pool resources and reach
- Explore the pros and cons of leading
- Assess the workload of leading the campaign before proceeding

Leverage someone else's platform

- Work with others to create online events to amplify reach
- Share data and contacts to mutually build businesses, especially yours

5

Managing the media

Case study: Call in the columnist

After many years of planning, development, and building, Phil, a large real estate developer, was finally ready to announce to the community what exactly was going into the prime retail space he had purchased, that also happened to be a cherished designated heritage building. As you can imagine, the public was very curious and so were the media. Throughout the stages of development, many reporters tried to find out what exactly was going to happen to the building. Getting attention for the announcement would not be hard given the intense interest in the project. Phil's company had already invested in building its own media network, which had thousands of followers on their social media, and thousands more on their e-newsletter subscription. But when it came to the big reveal, he decided to work with a popular and, at times, controversial columnist who had a keen interest in seeing development support the growth of the city, yet conversely, would also act as a scathing critic to the very developments he had hoped to see his beloved community thrive, so there was some risk involved, but a risk worth taking.

As we explored in Chapter 4, "Choose your channel", sometimes having someone else tell your story instead of telling it on your own within your own media network can be a beneficial strategy, and for Phil's real estate announcement, that is exactly what we decided to do. Working with the editor and columnist, we offered them the embargoed media release, project renderings, and inside information to provide greater context, and the publication would get the exclusive to share the story first with its readers in print and on their well-followed social media channels. As part of our negotiation, we would amplify the editorial coverage with sharing the announcement tools on the developer's own media network. As always, when working with the media, we knew there would be risk (more on that shortly) when giving up control of how the publication would present the story, but that is what the negotiation helped to assess, and we did our research. Both the publication and columnist historically supported developments like Phil's, and along with their physical distribution and immense social following, we took the calculated risk. We also negotiated that the feature come out on one of their most well-read days of the week to maximize distribution. The result was a positive full-page spread with a front-page cover image and a full-page section story. As it was first told by a well-established media outlet, social media engaged with the content robustly with thousands of shares and likes, and thousands of impressions and engagements as a result. Remember, one of the main reasons people use social media is to share news content, and we felt it was worth the risk to give up editorial control in exchange for the aforementioned. Furthermore, while mainstream media manages trust issues of their own with the public, there still remains a perception of if it's covered positively in the news, it must be a good thing, which can add value add to your earned media metric. In the end, the publication and the columnist got the coveted exclusive big story, and we received far more publicity than if we had simply gone out on our own media network.

A look ahead

In Chapter 5, we delve into one of the most impactful channels of amplifying your business storytelling – the mainstream media, whose own social media networks are in some cases more powerful than some of their own traditional channels. For Phil's development, showcased in the opening case study, the mainstream media amplification worked as part of the overall storytelling strategy. However, while a palatable storytelling option for Phil (and your business), Chapter 5 covers some of the risk and reward of working with the media.

Worth the risk?

Some of the world's largest brands have also forged some of the largest and influential "media networks", choosing, at times, to work with the mainstream media only to manage issues, and to make select strategic announcements as noted above. Need examples? Simply look at some businesses you engage with online, and it will not take long to see how telling the stories of their business, and the channels they chose to do so, has influenced, educated, or sold you on something or someone, or influenced you take an action. If your own media network has amassed a dedicated and robust following, would you risk losing control of the narrative for what may be only incremental additional media exposure with the mainstream media? Most of this chapter will explain why it is worth the consideration to work with the mainstream media to tell your story, and like anything project worth undertaking, it is also worth assessing the risk.

In its 2020 Trust Barometer Report, Edelman released its annual survey analyzing the trust and credibility in business, government, non-governmental organizations, and the media. For the latter, in North America specifically, trust in owned media dropped 6% from the previous year, with an 8% drop in the category of lacking a vision for the future.[1] Conversely, in the same category, trust in business was up 5%. I would like to suggest that businesses that have invested in telling their stories transparently, honestly, and effectively have contributed to this increase in trust, but that is only my deduction. See the endnotes for this chapter to review the full Edelman report. Trust challenges aside, the prevalent risk to working with the mainstream media is giving up control of how the story of your business is told once the journalists walk out the door. The risk is manageable, as I will share in this chapter, but it is not eliminated entirely.

The media is not a PR agency

Just because your business has successfully enticed a reporter to tell the story of your business, it does not mean you get a say in how that story is put together. To protect the trust of their institution, journalists must maintain some level of objectivity, and nothing will decrease trust in the journalist or the newsroom they work for than becoming a "mouthpiece" for the organization or business they are covering. In most, if not all cases, to achieve some semblance of balance, a reporter will seek out someone to provide an alternative perspective or comment, and most times, it is not in alignment with the narrative the story the business is hoping to convey. And, that's exactly what Phil read in the columnist's coverage, a variety of perspectives. However, no aspect of the coverage was surprising as we had identified detractors and enablers as part of our risk assessment prior to engaging the media. If you scan your local media every day, you will see many businesses that enter the media's daily coverage to tell their stories. If your story is well thought-out, transparent, and genuine, some balance from another perspective can make your story stronger in some cases as it has withstood the editorial scrutiny, and that builds trust for the media, and also credibility of the story of your business. As you can imagine, if you are not transparent, ethical, and most importantly prepared (understanding the media), your business escalates the level of examination by the media, which can cause irreparable damage to the authenticity of your story, and more importantly your business. Proceed, but proceed well-prepared and with a healthy dose of caution.

Media's agenda is often hidden

The agenda to tell the story of your business through the media is most often not the agenda of the media outlet you are working with. Before you pitch your story or decide to accept a media request to be interviewed as part of another story, ensure you are prepared by learning more about the media and the reporter, where possible. That information is at your fingertips with search engine results. It is also advisable to ask the reporter or producer you are working with about the treatment of the story and how it will be distributed. This simple search can show you the type of stories the reporter and media outlet prefer to cover and just as important, the tone in which those stories are covered.

Questions to ask

Some journalists tend to get defensive if you ask questions that appear to infringe on their ability to tell their stories objectively, such as, "can we see the final story before it is published?" That will not happen, as a general rule, with most newsrooms; however, you are still entitled to ask questions to assess if working with the media (and avoid any negative coverage) should be a part of your storytelling strategy.

1. What is the focus of your story?
2. Where and when will be story published, posted, and/or broadcast?
3. Who else are you speaking to? (Frame this question as helpful, and perhaps add "… so I do not risk duplicating information and answers".)

The last say goes to the media

Another risk to consider when working with the mainstream media to tell the story of your business is they almost always have the last word, even when they are wrong. It is their platforms after all, and should they make a mistake, my experience has been, most (but not all) media outlets will offer a retraction, but usually it is buried in the back pages of their publications or at the end of their broadcasts. And, if the mistake is egregious, prepare yourself for a fight, even litigious, if necessary, and even then, you may not get the retraction you're hoping for your organization. Again, on their platforms, they usually have the last say, but there have been legal challenges where some news organizations have been forced to offer their retractions on the front pages and lead off newscasts. Most businesses do not have the time or resources to have that fight.

If the media gets your story wrong, should you say something?

Well, it depends. As mentioned, most media outlets do not like to make mistakes, and then admit them, and you will need to assess how much damage is being done to your business's operations and reputation. If the mistake is very minor, I would let it go. That said, most editors I have known, present company included once upon a time, also care about the integrity of their editorial coverage, and would prefer to hear about all mistakes. As the saying goes, you catch more flies with honey than vinegar, meaning if you are going to ask to have a mistake corrected or story corrected, do so politely and respectfully, at least to start.

Too much of a good thing is a bad thing

In my broadcast journalism years, I led a newsroom, assigning and editing the stories our viewers consumed at the end of the day. During my senior editorial tenure, a new charity, very well-funded by private interests, came on the scene with a big, flashy media event, that in and of itself was enough to ask some critical questions, but the public will give a "pass" for an introduction. However, this event only served as a precursor to what was to come next, which was weeks and months of media releases, lavish events, and heavily produced content series – all to basically boast about the "good work" they were doing and how they could not do it without their partners in the private sector. It did not take long for our reporters to start asking some deeper questions, especially around financial responsibility given that it was a charitable entity, and soon other media outlets followed with closer examinations of their partners' interests, including some unflattering revelations that turned up through freedom of information searches. If your business has a great story to tell and working with the media to tell your story is part of your strategy, remember too much of a good thing can be a bad thing. That is not to say you need to hold back in working with the media but consider the pace and bravado in which you share and pitch your stories. Carl Radimer was my public relations professor at the University of Winnipeg. Sadly, Carl passed away in 2017, and while he may be gone, I am proud to able to share one of his (many) famous sayings that still guide me today: "Fifty percent of good public relations is staying out of the media."

Learning the landscape

Now that you understand some of the risks associated with working with the media, the remainder of this chapter will explore the benefits, along with what your business can do to work with the media to tell your story. If you have ever worked in sales, before you make the ask, an important part of the sales process is to undertake a greater understanding of your customer's industry. The media are no different, and it is why I advocate that before you pitch the story of your business, gain a solid understanding by learning the landscape in which the media operate, which is forever rapidly changing.

In the early 2000s, media convergence was like this massive conglomerate vortex that was absorbing dozens of media networks into a few powerful media networks. In Canada and the US, there are now currently only a handful of extremely large media entities that own and control most of the news and media services we experience today. For businesses seeking storytelling partnerships with the media, this has become problematic.

First producers and journalists who survive round after round of cuts following convergence or lack of ad revenue, they are expected to do more with less. In addition to producing daily assignments and special features, members of the media must now also keep personal social media accounts to interact with their audience and report live, sometimes multiple times a day. With such a heavy and demanding workload, that leaves little time to take calls and respond to emails from businesses like yours pitching stories. That said, any reporter that is committed to their craft will make time to explore a worthwhile story pitch. I will explain how to pitch your business story later in this chapter.

Each medium of media

Generally speaking, there are three traditional channels of communication for the mainstream media that now continuously feed their online platforms. In Chapter 3, I covered building your own media network. In this chapter, I outline the media's own network.

Television

In Chapter 4, "Choose your channel", I explained that traditional media, including television (both streamed online, via cable, and somewhat diminished over the airwaves) remains a priority choice for many people and how they consume their news and potentially the story of your business. The medium of television relies on video, audio, and words. In this chapter's case study, recall how we worked exclusively with the print columnist – the media outlet that employed him had a significant online following, and we produced a supporting promotional video, complemented by high-resolution imagery, both elements utilized in the editorial coverage. If you want to partner with television media to tell your story, ask yourself does your story provide the ability to offer meaningful imagery, audio, and written content? If not, television may not be the best fit.

Radio

As you would expect, radio is driven by audio elements. When developing your business storytelling plan, if the audience you are ultimately trying to reach is listening live, then radio is a proven option. Recall previously about a client of mine in the agriculture industry that produced podcasts for farmers who spent many hours in their machinery? For good measure, he also invested in radio advertising just to make sure he reached the "old timers" who don't stream podcasts, and there were many of them in his target audience. Radio content, just like television content, is also repurposed into media webpage articles.

Print

Of the three traditional mainstays, print media has suffered the greatest decline in subscription and advertising revenue. The cost of printing has become greater than the revenue and readers are also demanding more environmentally friendly options that do not include using paper and print products.

Website

Just like your own media network, the mainstream media anchors most, if not all, of its content to their websites, driven there by their support social media channels and content shared by others online. This content includes newscasts, stories from newscasts (maybe your business story?), repurposed content for webpage articles, and social media streams of the media network itself and their reporters. Given the aforementioned, just about every story the mainstream media considers producing must be suitable, at a minimum, for a webpage article as editorial content lives on media's websites.

Another trend to be mindful of with the mainstream media is more media outlets and networks are going exclusively online. They are abandoning the expensive "bricks and mortar" of physical locations, opting for virtual editorial meetings, eliminating expensive traditional production cost, and fighting to remain relevant with non-mainstream options that are growing rapidly in reach and influence. And, where traditional media are declining, they are shifting operations online – in many cases exclusively – hiring more online journalists who are multimedia trained and focused. For people who like to read the news, web-driven content is the preferred option, according to a 2018 study by the Pew Center, which found 63% of respondents read their news online over other options such as print and video.[2]

Social media

Just like you have discovered with your own media network, the media have harnessed the immense power and influence of social media and this is one of the top reasons to consider working with the mainstream media to tell the story of your business. The mainstream media have amassed large followings on their social media platforms, strengthened by the perceived credibility of objective sources of news having your story of your business covered by the traditional channels of mainstream media, complemented exponentially with their social media platforms. In addition to your own media network, it becomes evident just how much further your story is distributed when you can partner successfully with the media, which is what the case study at the start of this chapter also emphasized.

While social media also presents greater storytelling capacity, it also presents some greater risk as media outlets, already hyper-competitive, have even greater pressure to be first to post a story on their social channels. One of the more infamous examples includes when rumours that folk legend Gordon Lightfoot had passed away in 2010. "Reports" first surfaced on Twitter and spread like wildfire across social media and mainstream media. You could imagine Lightfoot's surprise upon hearing the news, and then having to participate in media interviews to confirm he was indeed still alive. Fortunately for the media that erroneously reported his "death", Lightfoot took it all in his stride.

Blogs and podcasts

Even though not traditional channels, mainstream media are embracing social media's auxiliary channels of communication. Their journalists and reporters, as part of their many other duties identified earlier, are strongly encouraged to write blogs and host podcasts, some of which have greater engagement with the media outlet's audience than the actual media outlet itself; another reason to consider working with the media to tell the story of your business.

Content producers

As mainstream media searches for means to stay relevant and viable, it is interesting to note that they have, in some instances, become content producers themselves, creating their own content production service. For example, for a fee, a media outlet will produce the story of your business for you. As you can imagine, this poses some journalistic conflict for the media itself. For example, dozens of current and former Canadian Broadcasting Corporation (CBC) employees are protesting this corporate content initiative as a conflict of interest between advertising and news, using strong language to make their point: "It's insidious. It looks and sounds like the news stories and podcasts we produce."[3] Stay tuned to see where this debate takes editorial storytellers next.

Non-mainstream is the new mainstream

While the demand for traditional media continues to shift and evolve, one underlying and motivating factor remains: people still want and crave news and information, and specifically in the scenarios offered throughout *Storytelling for Business*, they want stories. While larger media outlets continue to truncate, letting go many talented and experienced journalists, many of the departed are going out on their own, and in many cases, their readers follow them. A simple online search in your region will most likely turn up a handful (or more) independent media platforms, started by journalists and multimedia specialists. Their disadvantage is obvious: they do not have the legacy, history, and budget of their former employers; however, they do not have to manage significant expenses and have more editorial freedom. Additionally, as the independents grow in size and scope, they also grow in credibility, receiving coveted mainstream media access to many organizations like government, professional sports teams, and more. As mentioned above, with the demand for storytelling, many independent media outlets are circumnavigating the saturated advertising market with a dependable base of subscribers and/or those who pay through online crowdsourcing. Leveraging the power of independent media makes for another important channel of communication to tell your story.

How to pitch to the media

By this point in the chapter, my intention for your business is to have a firm grasp on the benefits and risks of working with the media. Restating, I do advocate, when beneficial to your storytelling strategy, that you find a way to work with the media to tell your story, but if the risk assessment is too great, then the decision is easy to utilize your own media network. If you have decided to pitch your story to the media, here are some tips to get you started:

Pitch directly to a journalist

One simple way to enter the media's agenda to potentially cover the story of your business is by pitching directly to a journalist. Before I go any further, "simple" does not mean easy; you will need to prepare before making that very important first point of contact. Remember, journalists get pitched to many times throughout their week. Think in terms of partnership: offer them a convincing story, and in return your business receives the benefit of their reach and distribution. At the heart of every great story is great people, and your story should connect a journalist to "real people", which I will share more in detail in our next chapter, "People Power". In the opening case study, we set up interviews with "real people" who'll benefit directly or indirectly from the development, anticipating the journalists will also find a few others independently, which they did, but they used our interviews predominantly. The point to drive home is, when possible, providing "real people" makes the story more palatable to the media. Through your research, find out what kind of stories the journalist likes to cover; follow their social channels; and determine their preferred point of contact. Many journalists post their direct contact info on their social media platforms or prefer to be contacted directly through their social media. Under the category of "small-but-very-important" detail, ensure you spell the journalist's name correctly. As you can imagine, with a last name like Wozny, there are many ways to spell it, and when I was a journalist, those who simply spelled my name correctly when pitching me stories of their business immediately had my attention.

Pitch the platform

One of the objectives for the explanations of mainstream media earlier in this chapter is to give you the right information to make the right pitch. Few things will kill your story pitch faster than selling a story that is not conducive to the media outlet's core competency. For example, if the only element you can offer up to the media to tell the story of your business is audio, then do not expect a video-oriented newsroom to cover your story. When journalists are assigned stories, they immediately think about what elements they need to tell that story. If your pitch provides those elements, you will likely have more success getting a reporter's attention.

Be responsive

After you make a pitch to a reporter, whether by email, direct social media message, or by a media release (see below), make sure you are available to field replies. Many companies make fantastic pitches, but fail to be responsive, and after a couple of tries, maybe a couple more if your business story is off the charts, the reporter will move on. If proactive, positive media coverage is the objective for the story of your business, you get more of what you give through reciprocity. Meaning, the more time and effort you put into providing meaningful supporting resources to the media, the more likely they'll use those elements (but not always), and remember how helpful you were in the process, which was a secondary objective in working with the columnist's newsroom.

Be prepared (for the response)

When developing the publicity strategy for any communication plan, the first thing I ask the client is "when you get the media coverage you desire for your business are you prepared to meet the demand?" For example, if your business sells a particular product, and the publicity push is to generate leads for the product, do you have the appropriate level of staff to meet the increase in calls from the public? Sharing again, getting decent media coverage is not always easy, and from a return-on-investment point of view, you owe to your business to maximize the investment in storytelling.

Tools of the trade

Media release

What's old is new again. That axiom certainly applies to the media release. Many businesses with communications departments or seasoned publicists have abandoned the media release in favour of putting the time and resources into bolstering their social media presence. In contrast, others see immense value in distributing media releases to the media and posting them to their own media networks, specifically their websites with a "news" section. I strongly support the latter. Media releases on webpages provide the perfect opportunity to increase the search engine optimization (SEO) of whatever it is you are attempting to achieve by telling the story of your business.

Media releases generally should be a full page, starting with the most salient information all wrapped up in the first paragraph. The next two shorter paragraphs include complementing information to support the opening paragraph with a quote or two, followed by contact information at the bottom. Keep your headlines short, with descriptive language and strong active verbs.

Backgrounder

One of the biggest mistakes some businesses make with their media releases is putting too much information on the first page. That is not to say extra information does not have its place, just as long as it is in the *right* place. Backgrounders serve media releases that may have a considerable amount of technical language or require greater explanations of policies and procedures. Backgrounders generally come after the contact information in the release and a link to the online version of the release as well. One page, two at the most (if truly warranted), will suffice for a backgrounder. Any greater in quantity and the story of your business presents itself as needlessly excessive. In the case study's example, we prepared both a media release and backgrounder, even though we gave the story exclusively to one media outlet. Given prior interest, we knew, even reluctantly after getting "scooped" by a competing media outlet, other media would assess the strong public interest, and cover the story regardless, though perhaps not as in-depth as the columnist who got the exclusive.

Media advisory

If telling the story of your business includes hosting a media event, distributing a media advisory separate from the media release is generally advised. The advisory's function is to advise on the who, what, when, and why, specifically names of people attending with the correct spelling.

Supporting content

Most newsrooms have strict policies to not use supporting content provided by a business that is telling its story. However, as shared earlier, with extreme deadlines and less resources to capture the elements of news, this strict "no use" policy has eased, even in some of the most ardent newsrooms. To get around the bending of their policies when using the content you produce for their editorial, most media outlets will provide note or credit indicating that the imagery or video was provided. The upside to providing your content is you control the visuals and have a greater influence on the narrative of the story of your business.

Editorial

An editorial is when an organization presents a firm opinion on something it is trying to influence. If the story of your business is to influence people to a call to action or make change in the community, a letter to the editor of a media outlet, traditionally a newspaper or a platform that relies on the written word, serves as an optimal storytelling tool. As always, before you submit your editorial, do your research. Most newspapers post their editorial criteria, including length, on their websites, and that they reserve the right to edit. Once again, when working with the media, they will almost always have the last word, and the editorial is another example. Review the media outlet's criteria before going through the effort to draft an editorial as stricter criteria usually applies to protect the integrity of their journalistic standard, which include word limits.

Advertorial

An advertorial is like an editorial except it is essentially a paid advertisement. What you pay for is what the media outlet will publish. However, to clearly differentiate between editorial and advertorial, media outlets will accompany your advertorial with the words "paid advertisement" prominently to indicate to their readers they are reading an advertisement. Advertorials have their merits, especially when you want to control the message.

Timing is everything

Timing is everything. This is yet another mantra to keep close when working with the media to tell the story of your business. Whatever tool or tactic you use to proactively engage with media, choosing *when* is crucial. Even though the news cycle is 24/7, most editorial meetings between senior editors and journalists occur early to mid-morning, giving intrepid reporters the days to flush out a story. As an expectation, journalists are expected to come to meetings with a story idea, which is not always an easy endeavour as there are many slow news days in a year. Using some of the tools and concepts shared in *Storytelling for Business*, pitching reporters early in the morning can work in your favour to get into the media's agenda as they scan other media and websites for story ideas. If their search turns up empty, your story idea may make the grade. Generally speaking, most journalists are always scanning for stories, and there really is not a bad time to reach out, but to be safe, avoid crunch times, which are usually late afternoons or during heavy news events, such as elections or other major breaking news. A well-known strategy for many public relations practitioners is to distribute unfavourable news late in the day on a Friday, at the end of the week. If you use a media release to tell the story of your business, that would be a timeframe to avoid, opting instead for distribution first thing in the morning, giving editors the time to review, and bring to editorial meetings. Furthermore, it never hurts to ask; in fact, I encourage in your planning and research, drop an email to the media outlets you are targeting to ask the optimal time(s) to send your media releases.

Media events

A media event is something you plan when you want to invite the media to a specific location for specific reason. For example, let's say your business is staging its grand opening of a new facility and you want to leverage the media for publicity, you would send out a media advisory to invite the media to your facility to see it them for themselves. A tremendous opportunity to tell the story of your business? Yes! However, without proper planning, your media event could make the news for all the wrong reasons. Below are a few important aspects of your event to keep in mind to get the positive media coverage you are aiming for while mitigating the negative media coverage you are not.

Location, location, location

An integral component of your media event plan should be the location. After all, the location showcases to the world the story of your business. If your media event includes speakers, depending on your location and how many people will be in attendance, you may want to consider a podium and even a stage to elevate the guests of honour. The media are your guests, and they come with expectations like proper lighting and audio, allowing them to capture quality audio and video, which is ultimately in the best interest of your business. Make sure the location of your event is easily accessible for the media. In particular, multimedia journalists come with equipment like tripods or other heavy gear. If they have lugged their gear a long way from where they park or up multiple flights of stairs, their state of mind and receptiveness to your product or service may be inadvertently reflected in their coverage.

If you want to celebrate something about your business that warrants a media event, most often that means an event at your actual business, and beyond just the location you select within your business. Advise your staff about media touring your facility, directing them to clean up their spaces, hiding away any sensitive documents and getting your business ready to showcase to the world.

Hospitality

Most media outlets reject hospitality and gifts as per the editorial policies to keep their journalists objective in their reportage. If you invite a guest to your home, what is one of the first things you do? You offer them a coffee, beverage, or some other expression of welcome. Your media event should be no different. As shared earlier, reporters experience extreme deadlines and the stress that goes along with it. While they may not say it, a warm coffee and some light snacks are appreciated. The same strategy can be said for small gifts, but anything beyond a token could be perceived as a bribe, even despite best intentions.

Expect the unexpected

Despite the best laid plans, just about every media event I have ever planned over the years has featured some unexpected or unwanted surprise, from inclement weather to uninvited protestors. No amount of preparation makes the unexpected any less stressful, but planning for the unexpected makes the difference between your media event covered as a good news story or a negative news story. As you plan your media event, invest the time to identify and mitigate any potential risks that could come up.

Worth repeating

Case study: Call in the columnist

- Consider working with a lead media outlet with significant online and traditional reach strategy to amplify coverage
- Work closely with reporter and newsroom, providing essential tools such as imagery, video content etc.
- Assess the pros and cons of working with just one media outlet exclusively
- Draft and distribute media tools, including a media release, if your story is of enough public interest that other media outlets will cover your story

Worth the risk?

- Assess the risk of working with the mainstream media, which includes giving up control of how the story of your business is told
- Understand if the risk is manageable, though never eliminated entirely, the reward is greater amplification of your story

The media is not a PR agency

- Remember, the media don't like to be taken for granted that they'll provide automatic positive media coverage
- Just because a reporter has agreed to cover your story, you will need to accept that the final article may not turn out exactly as you had hoped

Media's agenda is often hidden

- Ask questions to learn more about their coverage of your story
- Accept the last say often goes to the media, especially if the story is negative
- Assess that if the media gets your story wrong, should you say something? Sometimes, with minor errors, it's not worth the trouble

Too much of a good thing is a bad thing

- "Fifty percent of good public relations is staying out of the media" – Carl Radimer
- Present too many positive stories of your business and you'll most likely experience the opposite effect, which includes reporters wanting to take a look at other aspects of your business you'd prefer they not delve into closely

Learning the landscape

- Invest the time to understand the business environment in which the media work
- Know the media industry continues to face ongoing cutbacks and budgetary challenges

Each medium of media

Some key channels of mainstream media include:

- Television
- Radio
- Print

- Website
- Social media
- Blogs and podcasts
- Corporate producers

Non-mainstream is the new mainstream

- Give serious consideration to online and non-mainstream media that produce credible editorial and have grown in influence and reach

How to pitch to the media

- Pitch directly to a journalist
- Pitch the platform
- Be responsive
- Be prepared (for the response)

Tools of the trade

- Media release
- Backgrounder
- Media advisory
- Supporting content
- Editorial
- Advertorial

Timing is everything

- Consider *when* to reach out to the media if your intention is to get positive media coverage
- Understand there are certain times, dates, and events that limit your opportunities for getting media attention

Media events

- Choose your location wisely, ensuring it's also media-friendly
- Be hospitable, but don't cross the line into what could be considered bribery
- Expect the unexpected with every media event

6

People power

Case study: Dan's the man!

Anyone who has ever worked for a charitable organization knows that soliciting for donations and remaining relevant with stakeholders are done in an extremely competitive environment. Despite their meaningful and altruistic endeavours, charities must often work much harder than private institutions to stay operational and to grow, and they are competing among themselves, especially for the public's attention. As advertising budgets are generally smaller for charities compared to businesses, and certainly more scrutinized by their boards and the public, it is no surprise to me that some of the best storytellers for business are charitable entities. And the reason they tell phenomenal stories is because they have access to remarkable people, who on first impression, are generally immediately trustworthy and respected for working for such noble and altruistic causes.

Enter Dan, an affable and long-serving executive director of a well-known children's charity. The reason his charity is so well-known is because of Dan's tenure, stretching into its fourth decade. Ironically, in stark contrast to his larger-than-life appearance, Dan is about as introverted as they come, making his commitment to serve even more appealing to people behind the scenes who know and truly appreciate him. Strategically, two or three times a year, the charity Dan works for planned to enter the media's agenda to promote vital campaigns to generate donations, as well as keep the charity top of mind. Not to take all the limelight, Dan and his small team became experts to shine the spotlight on numerous volunteers, giving them all the credit for the outstanding results the charity achieved every year. From time to time, the media would also call on Dan to share his perspective on issues related to the less fortunate and vulnerable he served. Additionally, Dan has earned something of a celebrity status, with the media producing personal stories about him. With that celebrity and credibility comes influence, and Dan is often invited to be a guest speaker at high-profile events and serve on boards with other people of significant influence in the community. Naturally well-spoken, Dan harnesses some of the techniques I will cover in this chapter to help him succeed as a spokesperson, even though it is only a role he takes on because there is a direct correlation between the publicity and the influence, awareness, and donations his charity receives in return. Dan is the essence of people power, and it is people who are the essence of storytelling for business.

A look ahead

In Chapter 6, we shine the spotlight on the most important element of storytelling for business – people. For Dan, in the chapter's case study, even though he didn't like the spotlight, he knew he had the natural talent and supporting tools to benefit from the great good of calling his own number. Chapter 6 explains how to choose your storytellers, and how to prepare them to communicate your messages effectively and accurately, while coming across as genuine and interesting.

Dan's the man! (But not always)

As you read in this chapter's case study, Dan is indeed the man for the charity he works for, but as I alluded to, what also makes Dan and the charity he represents successful in garnering positive publicity is his ability to look around his organization and tap other people to tell their story. Dan understands the power of storytelling and how it connects his charity to all the important stakeholders that provide support – financial or otherwise. While Dan is the face of the charity, he does not have the best understanding of some of the impactful programs his charity organizes, which are run by a few dedicated employees and competent volunteers who bring expertise from other industries. When it comes time to tell the story of a specific program, Dan will shoulder tap one of his proven volunteers, following some media training, which I will cover later in this chapter. Using just one spokesperson to tell your story is a proven strategy where information may be sensitive or needs to be delivered with consistency, but if telling your story of your organization needs more technical input, bringing in a team member that possesses technical expertise builds trust as it demonstrates the other people who make your organization successful. Referenced in Chapter 5, Edelman's 2020 Trust Barometer indicates that among all the leaders you can bring forward, a company's technical expert ranks the highest, and that includes the company's CEO.[1]

Get real

"Real people" is a term I heard in a few iterations over my years working in journalism. Colloquially, it means avoid the people who officially speak for others. For example, instead of speaking to politicians to get their perspectives, connect with their constituents to hear their viewpoints, independent of what their political leaders say. Think about when you read a news story or watch a video about a business, when they feature people just like you, they tend to resonate because they are more relatable. As you plan to tell the story of your business, consider if your story comes across as more genuine if you include "real people" to share how your product or service made their lives better or influenced them to a desirable call to action. Careful not to overdo it on the platitudes or the story may seem like a commercial or sales pitch. When choosing "real people" for your story, keep in mind charisma does not always trump character or competency; meaning, "real people" do not often possess a slick on-camera presence or speak with a big, booming voice. They do, however, need to come across as credible, honest, and trustworthy, and with some of the media training tips below, they will have some tips and techniques to serve as interesting and influencing storytellers in the story of your business. Dan always did a thorough job of finding the right people in his organization for the right message, and he always made sure they were prepared and trained before sharing the organization's story publicly.

People peril

People are people, and that means we are not perfect, and we make mistakes, but for some people who are not prepared who tell your stories, that can spell disaster to your company's image and bottom line, both of which can take a considerable amount of time to restore. Take a minute to search "Tony Hayward BP Oil" online to see the disastrous fallout from the oil giant's chief storyteller at the height of an epic disaster. As mentioned and worth restating, mitigating any storyteller fallout should include closely analyzing your "real people" such as employees, volunteers, customers, or other people who benefit from your business or organization. They are fallible, too. I am not suggesting you form an interrogating committee to vet the people who assist in telling the story of your business, but it never hurts to truly assess your business ambassadors' skill and comfort level before you include them in your storytelling strategy. For what it is worth, I have yet to work with a spokesperson who is solely responsible for bringing down a company with their actions. Although some healthy caution is responsible, you can hedge your bet that a good spokesperson also makes for great storyteller for your business.

Influential intermediaries

An influencer means someone who uses their celebrity, expertise, and popularity to influence others, and more often than not they get paid quite well for their ability to influence. Dan certainly wasn't in it for the money, but he benefited from the influence. Meanwhile, although some social media industry experts assert that influencers flourish as a result of powerful social media channels, I would respectfully suggest "influencers" have leveraged their notoriety for centuries. Sure, the platforms have evolved over time from prehistoric pulpit to modern day social media platforms, but the ability to tap into someone else's ability to influence has remained an extremely valuable commodity. Influencers, like your business, have built their own media networks. The difference between the two comes down to the influencer wielding a far greater reach. For many businesses that want to tell the story of their business, they measure the time, money, and resources to create their own media network against the cost to retain an influencer's network to tell their story. The delta of influence between the two leads many businesses to hire influencers instead. Influencers have grown to encapsulate more than just your typical celebrity, including some we will share in this chapter. As part of his storytelling strategy,

Dan would often reach out to local, prominent radio broadcasters who supported his organization's cause, maximizing their status to showcase Dan's initiatives.

Influencers thrive by maximizing and complementing their social media following and influence. They use their social media and/or other channels like websites, blogs, videos, and more. Many kinds of influencers exist, and their reach, impact, and significance are growing in prominence every year. Here are some of the more common influencers, and I suspect you may know many others.

Celebrities

The term "celebrity" is broad, and it can include some of the references below, but I lead this section with this term to serve as a "catch-all" for the growing range of "celebrities" who count as influencers, which include niche influencers like inanimate objects or cartoon characters, or even memes.

Athletes

Athletes succeed on the world's stage in real time. We watch them thrive or overcome insurmountable obstacles, or in some cases, fail in spectacular fashion on live broadcasts or streaming services. Whatever the sporting scenario, some sports figures achieve hero-like status and profit greatly from it as they harness the adulation into their own powerful media networks, both with mainstream and social media. We look to them for fashion advice or other cultural recommendations like food or music, and in recent years, for statements about societal issues. Athletes' influence is enormous, far greater than the teams they play for. One study by Opendorse found that while posts from major league sports teams were more frequent than their athletes, their athletes posts' received engagement that was just over nine times higher.[2]

Creative types

Influencers I would categorize as creative types would include those whose creations have inspired thousands and millions to engage with them through their online presence or respond to the influencers' call to action. Most commonly, creative type influencers include musicians, actors, artists, and authors. Their originating platforms, such as movies, music, and artwork, connect with us in our homes, vehicles and other deeply personal space, which few people other than our loved ones have access to, making creative types extremely desirable influencers.

Politicians

Some politicians' abilities to excel as influencers is greater than others, but political figures can achieve extraordinary influence, building a huge following through their own media networks, with their social media as their base. Depending on what side of the political fence you stand on, US presidents, especially over the past two decades, have become the textbook case studies on how to wield political power to influence good or evil.

Pundits

Throughout *Storytelling for Business*, I have refrained, where possible, from naming names in order to avoid dating this book, and pundits serve as a good reason why – they come and go frequently. When they are in demand, they can carry incredible clout, serving on network news panel discussions, or their own content gets heavily consumed from their own media networks. Pundits cover the spectrum from mainstream to non-mainstream and generally stake their territory by offering commentary that stretches from insightful and experienced to caustic and controversial.

Industry experts

People who have a high degree of expertise in any field get sought out to share their knowledge and perspective. Some get so good at it that they leave their day jobs to benefit from the lucrative endorsements and speaking opportunities that come from companies who pay industry experts to influence customers to engage with the companies' products and services. In my view, the industry experts who do very well as influencers keep as much independence as possible, as they do not want it to appear their opinions can be easily bought and sold to the highest "bidder", and in the process, lose hard-earned trust and credibility from their followers.

Social justice advocates

Social justice advocates, sometimes more commonly, yet negatively referred to as social justice "warriors" (though I prefer advocates) can become overnight influencers given the speed in which social justice issues can dominate the public's attention, commonly borne from a dramatic event or circumstance. These influencers rise meteorically on social and mainstream media as the result of a social uprising, thrust into a spotlight as they demonstrate an ability to express their plight or viewpoints in a way that capture the public's attention. To maintain the public's influence, social justice advocates will pivot to create their own media networks to sustain their influence once the originating circumstances subsides or rises again at a later time.

Everyday people (like you and me)

Sometimes the most banal activities can generate the most unlikely influencers. As I am sure you have experienced, some everyday people have become outstanding at some unique skill or developed an in-depth understanding about something very few others have. As a result, their influence grows the longer they stay with it.

Animals

As humans, we possess an undeniable connection to animals. We depend on them for survival and companionship. For those reasons and others, animals have become influencers in their own right as their existence and purpose creates incredible storytelling. Storytellers of business will sometimes anthropomorphize animals to strengthen the emotional connection to their storytelling, as who can resist a cute puppy or fluffy kitten?

The issue with influencers

Little doubt remains, influencers can influence like few others can, which is why they get retained to tell the stories of businesses and organizations. While influencers come with the tremendous ability to shape opinion, they also come with tremendous risk to your business. Some influencers with proven track records come with a big price tag, eclipsed usually by their bigger personalities, which leave some businesses at the mercy of some influencers' mercurial personalities. Influencers are prone to controversy with little notice, which can run counter to the vision and mission of your business, creating "guilt by association". While active on their channels of communication, ironically, some influencers become very difficult to communicate with after the deal is done. And the managers or agencies who represent influencers can sometimes pose greater conflict than the influencer. An influencer contract that clearly spells out expectations and timelines can mitigate most concerns, but not all of them. By addressing issues with influencers at the onset of a storytelling partnership, the objective is not to dissuade your business from retaining an influencer, but rather to provide a starting analysis of the challenges and opportunities.

Call your own number

Whether as a lead spokesperson or influencer, you may decide "Hey! I can do this!" and I would encourage you to explore if you should call your own number to tell the story of your business. In the case study at the start of the chapter, recall how Dan, as an introvert, didn't easily embrace calling his own number, but for the greater good of his organization, and seeing its good work manifest in the community thanks to public support, he leaned in when necessary. Before you do, here are a few points to keep in mind as you make that assessment. Determine where you fit in the narrative of the story of your business. Are you a *real person*? Are you the official spokesperson? Are you the justice advocate or some other role? One of the main reasons to figure out your role in your business story is to estimate if you need others to augment your message or theme. For example, you may determine that the best way to tell your story is to spotlight your employee as a real person with you as the leader serving as an official spokesperson. Telling a business story with just one person usually comes down to the information shared externally. If the information is confidential or sensitive, then just one lead spokesperson who can provide a consistent level of messaging, along with performance, will give you greater control. This type of scenario is why you generally see just one lead spokesperson with large companies or organizations that manage sensitive information, like the police.

What you say is what you get

Once you have chosen and empowered your people to tell the story of your business, prepare them properly for sharing your stories publicly. Doing so is in their best interest and the best interest of your business.

Look and sound the part

After assessing, selecting, and preparing your storytellers, along with carefully crafting your key messages, invest the time and effort to look and sound the part. I have witnessed too many businesses create outstanding content but then fail to spend time on grooming their storytellers and spokespeople once they were in front of a camera or speaking on a podcast. For Dan, he placed a mirror on the back of his door, not out of vanity, but necessity to remind him to check his appearance before going on camera, as he did so regularly with the media.

As shared numerous times, people who consume your content will waste virtually no time on your storytelling if it is not compelling or the people presenting are not credible or are simply too much of a distraction. Sure, you cannot please everyone all of the time, and you will go insane if you try to, but the following guidelines will serve you as a storyteller if performance is required to tell the story of your business.

Get comfortable with being uncomfortable

Whether you or the leader of your business chooses to engage with the media or appear on social media, preparation is paramount, not only to navigate journalists' questions and counter-agenda, but to maximize your exposure to the public, and how the public sees you goes far beyond the written word I reviewed earlier. Accordingly, let's spend some time on how we can make you a better storyteller for your business with some simple techniques. For Dan, he was self-conscious about public appearances for storytelling, like most people are, and to get over his fear of looking and sounding "stupid", he committed to his performance. Like anything in life, the more time you spend on practising techniques to build confidence and skill, even if they make you feel uncomfortable, the better storyteller you will become on your own media network or the mainstream media's network.

Use your breath and your hands

If telling the story of your business puts you in front of a camera, avoid looking like the proverbial deer in the headlights (a phrase used for deer frozen in the middle of the highway as it stops to look into your vehicle's high beam lights). Less anecdotally, we have all seen someone on camera or being interviewed by a journalist who looks petrified to be there. To avoid that awkward exchange, which distracts from what you are trying to say, remember to breathe. Consciously remind yourself, breathe in, breathe out. This cue tells you that you can relax and think. My late uncle Al told the best stories. Even as I visualize him, it is not what he said that I remember most; it is how he told the stories. He used his hands to accentuate points and express strong points of view. As an aside, he was a very fast talker, and always amused us always with his playful yet confident assertion, "I don't talk fast, you listen slow". I am not suggesting you wave your hands frenetically as you tell your story to make your points, but practise expressing yourself using your hands and arms at key words and phrases.

Mind your body language

When my daughters were little, not a lot of time was wasted trying to figure out their moods when they sat slumped in their chairs, with slouched backs, furrowed brows, and arms firmly crossed. Yup, they were not happy about something, their body language said it all. If you are the lead storyteller, remember how important your body language is to the storytelling process. Before you appear in front of a camera take some deep breaths, clear your mind, and shake your arms out to remove any tension. Furthermore, keep the shoulders proudly back (not slouched), smile slightly, and more when appropriate. Put your best foot forward, shifting one foot or two directly to the source capturing your image or to the person asking the questions. Think about how you engage with people around you. If someone makes sudden, quick movements, that may make you feel cautious. Conversely, people move with purpose and deliberately generally convey a sense of trust, and that is the case if you are in front of a camera where the medium picks up subtle motions.

Related, one of the most common questions I get when coaching people to do media interviews is guiding them where to look. If it is just you in front of your camera, then the intent most likely is to speak directly to your audience, and you can achieve that outcome by looking directly at the camera, remembering the tips above. If the interview is host driven, I counsel clients to treat the camera as a "third person" in the conversation, as long as you know which one that is as some interviews have multiple cameras depending on the set up. If the host is speaking to the camera, keep your gaze on who is speaking, but reference the third person in the conversation out of respect. If you were in a conversation with two other people where one person was speaking to you, wouldn't it seem odd or maybe rude if the other person did not acknowledge your presence? If your interview is with a reporter with a camera, the journalist will most often direct you to look at them, and not their camera. The reason journalists make this request is to keep you from looking directly at their audience through the screen. Again, this treatment works if your intention is to speak directly to your audience on your own media network, but not for the reporter who is interviewing on behalf of their audience.

Be yourself

Whatever platforms you employ to tell the story of your business, credibility trumps charisma. As a storyteller or spokesperson, remember why you are there and the story you want to tell. This preceding sentence was at the essence of what made Dan incredibly popular and influential. Too many storytellers forget the "why" and feel they must be more of an expert or presenter than they really need to tell their story effectively. The big mistakes include over-emulating personality traits that are incongruent to their own. First and foremost, people who consume your content want to connect with people who are relatable, knowledgeable, and trustworthy. Your role in your story is to support the elements in the story with valuable messaging and perspectives that influence people to do something.

Dress and impress for success

Remembering that non-verbal cues have the greatest influence on how people feel about you, consider then that how you look can determine how you feel about yourself and how others see you in your story. There are a few things to keep in mind when your image is captured as part of your storytelling.

When in doubt, dress more conservatively. Avoid bright colours and patterns, and unless it is your own, do not wear any logos. If you wear complementing jewellery and make-up, keep it aligned with what you are wearing, and assess that it will not be a distraction. The same rationale goes with your hairstyle. In fact, your hairstyle can be the biggest distraction if too "out there", but I actually know many storytellers who deliberately go in front of cameras with memorable hairstyles by design. For them, the more outlandish the better as they say it is all part of the personality they want people to remember.

Grooming success

Over the years, I have had a few awkward conversations with lead storytellers about their grooming habits. Not everyone can carry off a few days of facial hair growth, and chipped nail polish does not come across well on camera when you are doing a show-and-tell with hand-held products. I think you get the point, but in case you do not, create a small network of people in your network who can provide some honest feedback about how you look before you go in front of a camera to tell your story.

Take on technology

By this stage of the book, I sincerely hope *Storytelling for Business* has prepared you to tell the story of your business, and if you do, whether you choose to embrace the technology yourself, go out-of-house, or work with media, at various points along your storytelling journey, you will have to take on the technology. When appearing in front of the camera or a mic, or both, remember technology is great when it works, until it does not. How many times have you been on a video conference call or webinar, or watched a live television interview when the camera goes down, mic stops working, or internet connection crashes, or all the above simultaneously? Obviously, when working with technology, and in a live environment, you cannot prepare for every breakdown, but researching and investigating on how to manage those circumstances, if and when they do occur, can save you a lot of stress and loss of credibility in storytelling situations gone sideways.

Air check? Check!

An old radio broadcasting term where you and/or your program director would sit together to listen to your on-air performance is called an "air check". At times, it was an excruciating exercise for me to sit there with my boss and review a less-than-stellar performance, but the best learning always came from the worst performances. There are two points to raise in this section. One, as shared often in *Storytelling for Business*, practice makes progress (not perfection), and two, as hard as it is to listen or watch yourself, you'll learn a lot from the exercise, and find an "on air" mentor to review as well. From experience I can tell you, you'll be pleasantly surprised how often people will say "yes" after you make a courteous and respectful request.

Air checks also help you to see how you performed with the technology you use to tell your story. For example, when Dan did live Q&A sessions on webinars, the supporting tools that came with the platform seemed like a good idea live, but when Dan and his team watch the recorded webinar back for review, everyone quickly realized less graphics was more, creating less distraction from Dan.

Worth repeating

Case study: Dan's the man!

- Recall how Dan, leader of a charity, used his people power to tell stories
- Understand that while not always easy, serving as a lead storyteller can yield many benefits

Dan's the man! (But not always)

- Explore other storytellers besides the lead or go-to storyteller

Get real

- Find people in your business who are "real people", not official spokespeople, but have direct connections to your products and services, and are relatable

People peril

- Realize all people are prone to mistakes during storytelling, but preparation and training can mitigate most risk

Influential intermediaries

- Influencers include: celebrities, athletes, creative types (musician, authors, artists), politicians, pundits, industry experts, social justice advocates and "warriors", everyday people, and animals

The issue with influencers

- Budget accordingly, as influencers can be expensive
- Learn to manage expectations as some can be hard to reach and have difficult representation
- Pose a reputational risk of "guilt by association" if their behaviour is suddenly controversial for all the wrong reasons

Call your own number

- Determine that sometimes the best influencer is you!

Look and sound the part

- Get comfortable with being uncomfortable
- Use your breath and your hands
- Mind your body language
- Be yourself
- Dress and impress for success
- Grooming success
- Take on technology
- Air check? Check!

7

Audience analysis

Case study: Access to audiences

As a community leader and advocate for the less fortunate, Alex had worked extremely hard for nearly a decade to get other community stakeholders to support her vision for a new shelter for the homeless in her city's downtown. The biggest challenged that remained for Alex and her team of advocates and supporters was they could not get the support of the local government to clear permits to build the shelter.

Deflated, but never willing to give up, Alex agreed to work with the community's business association, accepting the opportunity to present to the association's membership at their annual dinner about the need for the downtown shelter. The association had built up an impressive media network of its own and the annual dinner always received significant coverage from the media as many of the community's leaders and elite were in attendance.

While Alex had some trepidation about the event, fearing she would lose some control of the narrative, the annual dinner presented an opportunity she never quite had before – speaking unfiltered and unfettered to an extremely influential audience.

The event went remarkably well. Alex shined as she always does, steadfast in her conviction and beyond credible for her rationale to get the shelter built. In the 48 hours that followed, several influential bureaucrats within local government identified themselves and expressed gratitude and appreciation for the proposed shelter, offering their support. And, in the months following that one event, Alex and her team of supporters finally received the permits to demolish the building on site and start the process to construct the shelter. What was the difference this time around? And what made this event incredibly influential? The opportunity for Alex to speak directly to the public-at-large and out-of-reach stakeholders within local government through this third-party channel of communication (annual business association dinner) allowed her to have direct access to key people she hadn't before, albeit in front of a live audience. And, as the event was hosted by a credible third-party, Alex's presentation came across as genuine, articulate, and well-thought out and researched. She was their guest after all, and not the one potentially coming across as self-serving, seeking awareness for the proposed shelter.

A look ahead

Chapter 7 goes into greater detail about understanding who your audiences are when you tell the story of your business, how they could either be a friend or foe, or both, and as illustrated in the case study, you're most likely going to get more than you bargained for when it comes to exposure to additional audiences. While many other audiences exist, I have compiled some of the more commonly known stakeholders that may take a varied level of interest in the story of your business, whether it's through your own media network, the media, or both.

The most commonly known types of audience

Government

As the opening case study covered the potential of influencing government to tell the story of your business through a third-party intermediary (business association), let's start with government as a stakeholder group. If you want to influence government, engage the mainstream media, but do so with caution. Government, at all levels, watch everything the media does with an extremely hyper-critical eye. They will have in-house media monitoring services, hire out-of-house media monitoring services, or pay for both. Furthermore, the most senior leaders or the politicians themselves take interest in these types of reports, and if the story of your business includes engaging with government, they're going to know about it.

If you're trying to work collaboratively with government, you can see how this may not bode well for your organization. Imagine if Alex had heavily criticized the local government for not taking action; instead, she was pragmatic, sharing praise and appreciation for the dialogue. However, many organizations take very aggressive approaches to deliberately criticizing government through the media or on their own channels of communication. For example, an association representing thousands of members may expect or demand such action and pay big membership fees for that "loud voice". Government officials receiving that criticism are equally careful in their responses, as organizations represent many voters, and so the dance goes. If your objective is to create a collaborative relationship with the media, and you are going to proactively push your story on your network and the media's network, a good practice is to give your government contact a "heads up" about your planned activities.

(Other) media

In Chapter 5, "Managing the media", we discussed the media landscape and the intensely competitive environment in which they work, and the incessant drive to always be first to deliver or "break" news first. As the storyteller of your business, this time-sensitive dynamic can work to your advantage, as next to your government stakeholder, the media follow *other* media very closely. Most editorial meetings at the beginning of the day, and throughout, include an examination of what other media are covering. Senior editors monitor the social channels of other reporters at other news outlets, and if the story is significant enough, will shift their coverage to avoid being scooped. Strategically, take the time to determine if offering your story to one influential media outlet is better than sending out a release to all. As you read in Chapter 5's case study, we knew the story from our business was big enough to generate other media interest, regardless if one outlet told the story first. The media are tremendous amplifiers of stories, for better or for worse, most notably on their social media channels given the aforementioned. Much like working with government stakeholders, if your intention is to influence through the media, take a collaborative approach. When you present one media outlet an exclusive, as demonstrated in Chapter 5, keep your word to honour it, even if another media outlet gets wind that something is up. If you burn an exclusive, that reputation will follow you and your business the next time you need to pitch your story.

Employees

Employees are your most important stakeholder group, and that is why Chapter 9, "The inside story", covers internal storytelling. Whether on the job or after hours, your employees represent your business as the ultimate ambassadors, not to mention ideal "real people" as identified in the previous chapter. Employees are one of the few stakeholder groups that are influenced both internally and externally. Your employees consume news and are active on social media. What story you tell in the media or on your own media network externally, will be viewed by your employees as they have a tremendous stake in the well-being of the company they work for. Many of the businesses I have worked with over the years discounted their employees' response to stories externally or ignored them altogether, but over time we shifted their perspective to seeing employees as the most important stakeholder group to consider in any storytelling strategy, engaging them to have a say in the process, and serve as storytellers either in the actual story or when interacting with customers. Additionally, failing to keep employees close when developing your story, you lose out on maximizing your return on investment. Imagine you score some tremendous media coverage, complemented with a favourable response on social media, driving customers to your business. If your employees are not in lockstep with your story's message or not even aware, they will look uninformed and risk embarrassing themselves and your business, leaving your customer with a disconnected feeling between frontline staff and the company. When it comes to assessing employees as a stakeholder group, consider them a top priority as your customers typically interact with them first, and more often, then the leaders of your business. As your employees have more "face time" with your customers, they are your primary day-to-day storytellers.

Volunteers

As first identified in the previous chapter, "People power", if your organization relies on volunteers, recognize they are among the best "real people" to tell your story. What better way to demonstrate your support for a cause then to donate your time serving as a volunteer? If you have ever worked for a non-profit or charity, you know that volunteers are as passionate as your most dedicated employees. Accordingly, they take in your stories with tremendous self-interest. Like your employees, most volunteers define themselves by what they do and whom they volunteer for. When developing your storytelling strategy, carefully assess how your volunteer stakeholder group will respond to the story you are telling. Keep them close and share plans where possible. Most importantly as "real people" or spokespeople in your story, prepare them well before sending them in front of the media or empowering them on social media – make it clear what they can say and cannot say, and prepare them to deflect tough questions that are outside of their volunteer duties back to leaders of the organization. Journalists, at times, will try to get a volunteer to speak for an organization, but it's unfair to expect a volunteer to act as a spokesperson if they are not prepared, not to mention the potential damage a few wrong statements can cause.

Customers

Customers as a stakeholder group is quite broad because it requires a deeper dive into what kind of customers and where you as a business hope to engage them during your storytelling journey. When you build your storytelling plan and distribute the story on your own media network, constantly examine which customers are you targeting and when. Does your story go after new customers or existing customers, and how are they going to respond to the story you produce or the coverage they see on their favourite media outlet? Along with understanding your customers' demographics, invest in some worthwhile time to understand your customer's psychographics (covered in greater detail in this chapter). By analyzing both demographics and psychographics, you gain a greater appreciation for how your customers will respond to the story of your business, which can set you up for a greater return on investment, eliminating the guesswork of what your customers want to experience with your storytelling and what treatments and elements (Chapter 2, "The story behind the story") resonate most with them.

Donors

Depending on your life's priorities, time is more valuable than money or vice versa. Either way, both represent the ultimate commitment to your organization's very survival if you rely on donations. As a stakeholder group, many donors double as volunteers, and their stake in your organization is deep rooted. For non-profits and charities, making donors their number one stakeholder group makes sense as they plan, execute, and distribute their stories externally.

Suppliers

When it comes to suppliers for your business, your success is their success. Sure, they appreciate your business – and keep in mind, your suppliers have access to your business operations more than your customers or public does. In some ways, your suppliers are your auxiliary employees, so to speak. If you don't succeed as a business, your suppliers won't succeed; therefore, they serve as champions and have a vested interest in the story of your business, and to amplify that message through their channels of communication as they want to be associated with your story to indirectly promote and tell theirs.

Investors and lenders

Many businesses get off the ground only because of funding from investors and lenders who believe in them. My experience has been they generally want to remain in the background and prefer not to step into the spotlight of your story, but there are always exceptions, of course. Nonetheless, much like suppliers, they are keenly interested in seeing your business succeed and will keep tabs on your progress online. As you construct the story of your business, consider how this vital stakeholder group will receive the sentiment of your story. Moreover, if your lender and investor approach you to tell your story through their own media network, give it some serious consideration as their networks are often robust and well-resourced.

Special interest groups

One stakeholder group or audience that is overwhelmingly underestimated compared to all others mentioned in this section of *Storytelling for Business* is special interest groups. In my experience, they can sometimes be the difference to supporting or deterring a project or initiative that your business is trying to achieve and influence by the story. Special interest groups are generally made of passionate and driven volunteer members who come with their credible professional backgrounds as lawyers, doctors, accountants, and so on. When mobilized, a special interest group can develop powerful networks in little time and secure funding from a number of unknown sources, along with keen and sympathetic interest from media. I have witnessed special interest groups take businesses and government all the way to the supreme court or I have experienced special interest groups align their interests with that of an organization or business, all for a common goal. What catches most organizations off guard with special interest groups, is they almost always never see them coming once a story is posted or published. Furthermore, for self-interest purposes, some special interest groups will outright target a business with a considerable media network and influence to move their interest along, and in the process garner a lot of media and social media attention, often void of context and little accountability. I've grown to call this activity by some special interest groups "negative affirmation". The irony with a successful storytelling organization is that the more success they achieve, the more risk they assume for having their brand leveraged for potentially nefarious purposes.

Think of the narrative of your story: are there any issues or cause that might flag a special interest group? If so, invest some time into research what groups exist, and to what level they engage – either negatively or positively.

Social media influencers

In Chapter 6, "People power", I covered the impact social media influencers have with immense audiences. As you produce the story of your business, you may not be considering influencers as part of your strategy for any given reason, including budget. That's not to say influencers won't engage with your story if they sense some meaningful connection. A simple search engine scan will usually uncover numerous celebrities commenting on a product or service of a small business that shoots that business out of relative obscurity into the mainstream, with the sales to follow. Conversely, social media influencers also hold institutions and businesses to account if they feel the story is sending the wrong message. What usually follows is the influencer's loyal followers piling on, and the business suddenly finding itself in a crisis (more in Chapter 8), rather than just managing a storytelling strategy. It is unlikely your story will catch the attention of a high-profile influencer, but it does happen from time to time. Much like with special interest groups, take the time to examine if the story you're telling for your business will inadvertently get in the crosshairs of any influencers. And by the way, some companies strategically create stories and content with the intent of engaging influencers, both for positive and controversial exposure, depending on the subject matter.

Getting graphic!

Two of the most important words for analyzing audience are *demographics* and *psychographics*. Demographics essentially explain who your audience is, or at least, gives you some clues. Psychographics essentially explain what influences your audience to do something. In the context of telling the story of your business, getting to know your audience and what they like or dislike will guide you as you develop and create your storytelling for business strategy. Alex considered both when deciding to participate in the association luncheon. By assessing the demographics and psychographics of her key audiences, she knew they would most likely be attending based on data provided by the association. In the end, the research was accurate, and Alex finally got in front of some influential stakeholders as a result.

Audience demographics

Age

Understanding the age of your audience can help you select what channels of communication they might prefer. For example, the success of social media platforms is fleeting, and what may be popular with the kids today may be out of style tomorrow, or what channels adults like, simply by sheer defiance, may not be what younger age groups prefer.

Gender

Of all the key demographics to consider, my experience has gender as one of the more impactful. Working in professional sports for over five years, never did I see such polarity in popularity when it came to content. What content male audiences preferred to consume was usually in stark contrast to what female audiences preferred, and that carried over to when and where they preferred to experience the content. If your business needs to tell a story to a specific gender, you could see how you might miss the mark on a large segment if the storytelling elements used repel rather than attract that gender.

Marital status

If you think about the trajectory of your own life, you will know that what influenced you five years ago was different than say ten years ago, and that's amplified depending on whether you are married or have a long-term partner. Perhaps no one person has a greater impact on how your audience views your contact than your "significant other".

Income

If the primary objective of your storytelling is to sell something, understanding the role of income can make or break if your product or service ultimately sells. For example, if your business sells a niche luxury product and you tell your story through channels used by demographics that can't afford it, not only will you risk seeing little return on your storytelling investment, you also risk getting ridiculed as "tone deaf" when it appears you have no clue who you're telling your story to.

Ethnicity

If your storytelling embraces elements to influence or heighten specific aspects about culture, ethnicity will play a prominent role. Ethnicity has its own unique characteristics and traits, and lends itself to meaningful storytelling as it's authentic. Where things can go sideways is if your storytelling exploits that culture to sell or influence, or even has the appearance of doing so.

Diversity and inclusiveness

With a greater understanding of your audience demographics comes the added responsibility and what many advocates say is also the responsibility for business storytellers to incorporate a genuine expression of diversity and inclusion (D&I). As shared in previous chapters, the people that matter most to your business are looking for corporate social responsibility (CSR) initiatives in your storytelling and are also looking for content that demonstrates your openness and inclusivity – to everyone. Many definitions of D&I exist, but at its core is recognizing and acknowledging we are all different and empowering that diversity to have greater representation. The term *equity* also plays a role in D&I storytelling with the narrative of opportunity and fairness, a common theme among human resources professionals, who in turn lean on business storytellers to create content – both for external use to recruit employees and internal use to keep them.

D&I is reflected in the storytelling elements you use and the people who tell your stories. For example, most major dictionaries define *binary* as including two things or two parts, and *gender binary* traditionally means male and female. *Non-binary* includes people who don't exclusively identify as male or female, and may employ pronouns such as "they" instead. If your story's objective wants to portray a sense of overall inclusiveness, using *just* gender binary pronouns "he" and "she" will most likely have the opposite desired outcome. In your business storytelling, do the elements you choose, including storytellers (people) reflect a diverse and inclusive business? If not, should they, based on knowing your audiences?

As with all storytelling for business projects, they should be measured against company objectives, and D&I checks a lot of measurement boxes. From experience with client and company internal research on assessing the D&I and CSR initiatives, it wasn't surprising to learn inclusive cultures are more likely to meet and exceed company goals such as financial targets as well as creating a healthier work environment that produces a greater quality of work. As a business storyteller, communicating diversity and inclusion is not only responsible, it's good for business.

Audience psychographics

With a better understanding of who your audience is with some key demographics identified earlier, let's look at what influences your audience to do something, specifically related to the story of your business using psychographics. Here are some of the more commonly referenced psychographics and how they can relate to your storytelling endeavours.

Activities (social behaviours)

What your audience does most with its time can and does correlate with meaningful engagement with your story. For example, if you want to influence people to purchase a line of products, understanding how they might use them, and how often they might use them would be valuable information as you plot out your story.

Attitudes/opinions

If one certainty presents itself above all psychographics it is that your audience always will have an opinion about something. Conversely, with that certainty I have found it remains one of the hardest psychographics to tap into as many people hold their opinions and attitudes as sacred – and sometimes very confidential. If you can identify key opinions and attitudes from your audience, your story has a greater chance to succeed as people generally seek out information and content that supports their own opinions, known as confirmation bias. For Alex, in the opening case study, her story was well received at the association event by the majority of people in attendance, creating social proof among those who were there to shift their perspective to back her project.

Values

Some of the most successful storytellers in business have succeeded where many others have failed because they clearly established values as stories within the overall narrative of the company. For some businesses that means, by way of example, sustainability. Even before their products hit retail, they've undergone rigorous testing to ensure they leave minimal waste in the environment from purchase and packaging to eventual disposal, and the business that invests significantly in sustainability also invests just as much, if not more, to tell the world about what they're doing to keep the planet green. In return, audiences who align with stories like this return the favour by becoming loyal customers and product advocates.

Lifestyles

What often defines many people is their lifestyle. For many people, how they choose to live has become the most primary form of storytelling and one of the lead tenants to why social media has thrived. There's a saying I'll paraphrase that goes something like, "some people buy things they can't afford to impress people they don't like". Influencers have done very well by simply telling their stories by how they live their lives, complemented by the products and services that make life great – real or perceived.

Geographics

With a better understanding of demographics (who's your audience) and psychographics (what influences your audience), the next step in your audience analysis to tell the story of your business is to know where your audiences live. Thanks to technology, mainly social media's rich data collecting platforms, finding where your audiences live and how they live has never been easier. There are four areas to analyze where your audience lives and works.

Local

If your audience is local to your business, your storytelling will reflect the demographics and psychographics primarily the closest to you. As an advantage, assuming your business is also local, you will spend less time and resources trying to learn more about other areas outside of your market.

Regional

Even with the internet's powerful e-commerce capabilities, most businesses start locally and sustain themselves by growing regionally. Not surprisingly, the further your audience is away from you, the more effort is required to reach and understand them. Generally, a regional audience is not entirely different from your local audience, but nuances in demographics and psychographics start to become more noticeable.

National

The national audience is yet another much larger area outside of your regional audience and another level up from your local audience. The national audience is where your business will truly experience the expanse of demographics and psychographics. For example, in Canada where I live, a very large country, people are very different in many ways depending on where they live. Canada's a bilingual country (English and French) and for many storytellers wanting to appeal to a Canadian audience, developing two parallel stories in both official languages is required, not to mention entirely different psychographics, even within the same country borders. Factor in Canada has other predominant languages represented in our First Nations, and your business can see why analyzing your audience's geographics becomes as important as demographics and psychographics.

International

As shared in Canada, language is just one significant challenge (and opportunity!) for storytellers for business to contemplate. Now, imagine how that challenge is exponentially greater in

Europe where several other neighbouring languages and cultures are prevalent. As a business storyteller, in say, my country, I have now added yet another level up from my starting local audience. At this point, if my storytelling needs to require an international presence, my need to undertake a more involved audience analysis has become absolute essential or I risk diluting my messaging and desired objectives with more audiences and their demographics and psychographics. The point here is not to overwhelm you, but to enlighten you about the breadth of audiences as they relate to the geographics in which they live, work, and play.

Digging up data

Demographics, psychographics, and geographics. Sounds like some very technical information that requires a big investment in time, resources, and money, right? Yes and no. Most countries have their own publicly shared databases, rich with some key demographics and geographics, curated from annual census campaigns. Government, much like your business, needs to tell stories, too, and bureaucrats need to know specifically whom they're telling stories to and where their audiences live. That's why in many countries, completing a census is a mandatory civic duty. If you're obligated to participate, why not benefit from the data as a business storyteller? In Canada, we have Statistics Canada (www.statcan.gc.ca), which I referred to a few times in previous chapters, and in the United States curated data and statistics are posted on www.usa.gov and www.census.gov. Additionally, some private data collection agencies will post free insightful reports, designed to get you to pay for their services, some of which include more contextual analysis behind the stats government services provide for free.

One of your best sources of free data to find out where your audiences are coming from is your own media network. Your website, your main storytelling tool, and your channels of communication, your social media channels, all come with robust data collection back-end platforms. By way of example, social media giants' curation of your audiences' habits and interactions with your business online is so robust, many social media consultants make a good living providing the service of doing data deep dives, if you require in-depth analysis, and many storytellers do if they require reaching a very specific audience and very specific location.

Email, that tried-and-true channel of communication, provides tremendous audience analysis data, which I'll cover in greater detail in Chapter 10, "Making measurement matter". In the meantime, even the most basic third-party email newsletter programs provide rich data analysis of where your audience is opening your email from, when they opened it, and what they did after they opened your message.

Take a look around

As simple as this sounds, where applicable, have a look around. Start with going physically to where your audience or customers live, work, and play. For example, if you sell swimwear, go to the beach and people-watch, respectfully. If you look with intent, you'll be pleasantly surprised what informative patterns and habits you see that can translate into the development of your story. Furthermore, if you have permission in a public place and you're not bothering anyone, you could attempt to construct a short survey to curate your own data.

What your competitors are doing

Imitation is the sincerest form of flattery, as the saying goes. When you succeed in telling your story, I guarantee you that other business storytellers are going to carefully look at your content, taking away what works for them, and building the elements they gleaned from your story into their content. While never plagiarising someone's idea outright, check out what your competitors create for effective storytelling.

What your industry is doing

From your competitors, look around at what your industry does to tell stories for their businesses. Big or small, creative content does not discriminate based on the size of the business. Organizations, like associations, for example, that represent companies similar to yours offer a fulsome resource of storytelling for business ideas. Furthermore, you can create environmental scans where you document the other businesses you visit, along with detailed notes and observations about what you're experiencing when you consume your competitors' storytelling content. Environmental scans provide some good data, most compelling I've found is patterns of storytelling elements that their audiences engage with or disengage with because perhaps they've been overused and used ineffectively.

What other industries are doing

Confirmation bias means we seek out information and perspectives that closely resemble and support what we believe and value, and that way of thinking is most prevalent in storytelling for business. I confess, I have been guilty of confirmation bias as a storyteller and communicator over the decades, simply out of comfort and ease because I'm busy like all other storytellers. Without hesitation, some of the better storytelling ideas I have experienced have come from exploring industries completely out of my circle of knowledge and expertise. In fact, I find looking at completely different industries challenges me to look at storytelling elements in ways I never have before, and as a result, facilitates absorbing creative new storytelling tactics, along with innovating what I have relied on for many years.

Seek outside counsel

When assessing your audience's potential response to your story or who will view it in the first place, consider securing an experienced perspective if your own research has not yielded the results you were hoping for or found the data you need. With every step of developing your story, start with clarity to get maximum results. If you need to retain an out-of-house research and data firm, the more specific you are with your storytelling objectives, the better your chances are for them getting you what you need to tell your story to the right people, at the right times, and in the right locations. And you will save time and money, as the agency will spend less time (billable hours) getting the information it needs from you to dig up data. If you're on a budget, and many business storytellers are, consider some very trusted creative types within your network you can trust to provide honest and valuable feedback.

Create personas

When working with clients to create training content, I will get whoever has been designated to read the introductions to video on camera, using a teleprompter, to visualize they are only speaking to just one customer who represents all customers in their audience. Also known as an avatar, the advantage of thinking about your ultimate customer persona is you'll need to carefully review and analyze the demographics, psychographics, and geographics shared earlier. Furthermore, throughout the storytelling for your business process, you will have a touchstone or North Star, to guide you along your story arc.

Worth repeating

Case study: Access to audiences

- Consider third-party opportunities that give you exposure and access to influential people to tell your story

- Research audiences in advance to shape your messaging and presentation to maximize influence

The most commonly known types of audience

- Government
- (Other) media
- Employees
- Volunteers
- Customers
- Donors
- Suppliers
- Investors and lenders
- Special interest groups
- Social media influencers

Getting graphic!

- Demographics – who your audience is
- Psychographics – what influences your audience
- Geographics – where your audience lives

Audience demographics

- Age
- Gender
- Marital status
- Income
- Ethnicity
- Diversity and inclusiveness

Audience psychographics

- Activities (social behaviours)
- Attitudes/opinions
- Values
- Lifestyles

Geographics

- Local
- Regional
- National
- International

Digging up data

- Access valuable data on graphics from both paid and free sources, which are equally insightful

Take a look around

- Understand what storytelling content your audience is consuming
- Check out your competitors' content
- Look around your industry and non-related industries
- Seek outside perspectives

Create personas

- Develop what the ideal person who matters most to your business looks like and create content to suit their preferences

8

When a story goes
sideways

Case study: When a story goes sideways

As a fourth-generation owner of his family business, Erick had to work incredibly hard to earn the trust he enjoyed in the business community, proving that he possessed the character and competency to run a manufacturing company with 3,000+ employees that his great-grandfathers started close to a century ago. Naturally, Erick was the obvious choice to celebrate a major milestone in the ongoing success story of his company – the opening of a new facility.

Telling this story of Erick's family business had been a successful months-long campaign, complete with all kinds of interactive content shared on the company's own media network and amplified through the mainstream media. While Erick didn't embrace the spotlight, the spotlight sure embraced him, as Erick commands a folksy, easy-going demeanor that the "average Joe" could relate to.

The milestone event was *supposed* to be just another, in a long series of successful publicity and community relations events, led by Erick that started with the traditional ribbon-cutting ceremony, greetings from dignitaries, and ending with closing comments from Erick himself.

Erick was a consummate leader and spokesperson, sticking to the script, but adeptly weaving in careful commentary and stories off-script, which was what made him appealing to the company's stakeholders. As Erick worked his way through his script, he included some carefully curated cultural comments (or so he thought) about a minority group of customers that he had a tremendous affinity for as they demonstrated the company's commitment to embracing diversity, innovating their products for a variety of growing ethnic backgrounds. In the immediate hours that followed, the company's opening event for its new facility, the online commentariat took umbrage with one of Erick's comments, specifically how he "inaccurately and insensitively" used offensive terminology to describe the culturally appropriate garments one minority group wore when he visited them in their workplace. Offending anyone, most specifically his valued customers, was the last thing Erick wanted to do, but social media did not relent, pounding the company's social media handles, demanding an apology, even suggesting his removal as the head of the company.

With meticulous planning and a well-executed campaign to tell the story of Erick's business, the story had suddenly gone sideways and into unexpected crisis communications mode. Yet, in just 48 hours after the story went fully sideways, Erick was able to turn the deluge of negative social commentary from a downpour to merely a sprinkle that would dry up a just few days afterwards.

First thing the next morning after the "big event", figuratively and literally, Erick, who himself, was genuinely taken aback by how his comments were interpreted, accepted that even though his intention was not to offend anyone, he clearly had, and he had to take immediate responsibility. He called the group he offended, offering his heartfelt apology, and committed to never attempting to share sentiments about cultural awareness without first ensuring his comments were vetted by the appropriate cultural leaders. While hurt and admittedly disappointed in Erick, the group's leader accepted his apology. As a leader of action, and Erick felt compelled to back up his words and demonstrate his commitment to the group. With a small group of his company's leaders, Erick discreetly went to visit the group he offended later that morning with a donation to contribute to three scholarships for students within their community. They graciously accepted. Additionally, Erick accelerated his leadership team's upcoming diversity and inclusion training, which they had already invested in a first session and shared his plans with the group he visited. When Erick got back to the office, his team released a statement from their own media network and to the media that humbly apologized for the inappropriate references and a demonstrated commitment to learn from the experience, and further advised that Erick reached out directly to connect to the group to share his apology. Concurrently, a statement to the employees was distributed that same morning through internal channels of communication, offering an apology for misrepresenting the company "we all hold sacred", sharing how he reached out to the group that was offended, and that an offer of reconciliation had been made and accepted.

Externally, still upset with the insensitive comments from Erick, the intensity of the social media backlash went from intense to tepid within 24 hours, satisfied that the apology was sufficient as it was transparent, trustworthy, and timely.

In the weeks following the "event", Erick and his leaders followed up with the group, extending internship opportunities for the bursary winners, and seeking feedback on how to best build relationships within their group and others. The overture was again well-received, turning once ardent detractors into appreciative champions of Erick and the company.

A look ahead

Chapter 8 guides you through how to respond and recover if the story of your business does not go as planned, generating a negative response, or inadvertently harming the operations of your organization. As carefully presented in the Chapter 8 case study with Erick, he did manage to recover relatively quickly, but respectfully, not all businesses have leaders who have the capacity to pivot as Erick did so effectively. While avoiding a sideways story like the Chapter 8 case study is not always possible, we cover some strategies to prevent sideways stories from occurring in the first place and who you need on your team to help you with this important risk-mitigation strategy.

Things don't always go as planned

As you've read in the story of Erick's family business, the best laid plans to tell a story can go sideways quickly. Understandably, no business communicator deliberately goes out of their way to have their story go sideways, but when it does happen, and occasionally, it will happen, understanding how, what, and with whom to set the story straight can mitigate any damage to your company's reputation. As many famous quotes from experienced leaders have intimated over the years, it can take decades to build a successful business, but only minutes to tear it all down if a crisis is not managed in a timely, trustworthy, and transparent manner. At the core of when a story goes sideways, is when you as the storyteller, have lost control of the narrative by some unexpected event or circumstance, and to get your story back on track, there are four T's of taking control for you to consider: transparency, trustworthiness, timeliness, and technology.

Transparency

What your stakeholders want from your business when the story goes sideways is transparency, avoiding subterfuge, and how you'll fix what is wrong. If you're genuinely wrong in the circumstance, say so, and say sorry if necessary. As with Erick's sideways story, while it wasn't intentional, he accepted responsibility and took action to reach out to the group he offended. He apologized and went above and beyond by offering bursaries to students within the group's community, not as a public relations exercise, but as it was the right thing to do to rebuild the relationship, which he succeeded in doing, in fact stronger than ever. He also created an action plan with his leadership team, and communicated internally to his employees the apology, overture to the offended group, and action plan referenced in the case study.

While not necessarily applicable to this chapter's case study, some other points to keep in mind to prevent your story from tipping further sideways include that it's okay to not know the answers at the start; the important thing is that you're communicating to your stakeholders and not hiding from the issue. Where a sideways story can get only worse is when spokespeople speculate on answers when they themselves don't know. Every time I put a spokesperson in front of the media, I review with them the media relations protocol to never speculate if you don't know the answer, and then remind them again just before they speak. In the nascent stages of a crisis, information is lacking, juxtaposed by an intense demand for answers by a company's stakeholders.

Indirect vs. direct accountability

Depending on the circumstance, it's also okay not to offer up a response, especially if that circumstance doesn't require you to be accountable. For example, let's say an environmental disaster dramatically disrupts your operations, along with many other businesses in your industry; that is an indirect event. That said, always checking in with your Touchstone Team (explained in greater detail later in this chapter) as an opportunity to reassure stakeholders can prove beneficial, even if the inquiry is as a result of an indirect event. Direct accountability is when an event or circumstance is the direct result of something your business is responsible for. In Erick's case, he was directly responsible for the comments that created a tremendously negative response, and as a result, his company had little to no choice but to respond, which is the right thing to do.

Trustworthiness

When your story goes sideways, your stakeholders have taken a "withdrawal" from the "trust account" they have invested in with your business. How trustworthy your response is and your performance as the storyteller will ultimately determine if they "re-deposit" their trust or "spend" it elsewhere if they're ultimately not satisfied.

Start with words, finish with action

Whether speaking directly to stakeholders and/or in written communication, what you say is just as important as how you say it. Choose your words carefully. Avoid words that are puffery in nature, choosing instead simple, matter-of-fact language, that provides direction and commitment to resolving the issue or event that cause the story to go sideways. If people are negatively affected by your story, recognize them first and foremost. In the case study, I shared Erick apologized directly to the group he offended first privately and then publicly. For most leaders embroiled in a story that has gone sideways, they genuinely didn't intend the narrative to go negative. In crisis mode, the goal is not to make it better, as the damage is already done, just try not to make the situation worse, and how a leader or business responds can make matters significantly worse if not done carefully and correctly. For example, if a leader complains about how hard the circumstances have been on them personally. Your stakeholders are more concerned about those who have been negatively impacted. If you, as leader, get asked "how are you doing personally?" and many reporters will ask this question, it's always a wise approach to deflect the response back to making sure those who have been affected remain the priority.

Do the right things for the right reasons

When re-establishing trust when a story goes sideways, aim to do the right thing for the right reasons. For Erick, while sharing his apology externally and internally was important, it was equally important to rebuild the relationship with the group he inadvertently offended with more than just words. When offering a contribution to their scholarship fund, it was done with the intention of demonstrating a commitment to reconciliation for his actions. The company's objective was to right a wrong, and as a result, they re-established trust with the group, and it also created advocates for the company who spoke favourably about the outcome of the story that went sideways.

Storytelling after it's gone sideways

However you choose to tell your story after it has gone sideways, when it comes to "how", consider the following principles. Earlier I drew the analogy to your audience withdrawing from the trust account and they're willing to re-deposit their trust, watching closely how you respond. They're looking for your business to be clear and confident in its response, but not too overconfident.

Speak or respond in a calming manner, remaining empathetic where and when the situation calls for that tone of response. Keep your language simple and not excessively emotional as the situation that got your story to go sideways is most likely already emotionally charged and doesn't need any more of that energy. If the result of your story going sideways has people hurt or offended, how you respond should include responsible language and action that is directed at them, and not necessarily about your company or you as the storyteller. As always, exceptions exist to any rules; for example, employees and other internal stakeholders may have been directly or indirectly impacted, and it may also be necessary to acknowledge their concerns.

When the story of your business goes sideways, the hours and days afterwards, if it gets that far, can be some of the most stressful your company ever experiences, and the temptation and "easy way out" will present itself to shoot the messenger, like Erick. Unless the response or originating action is so egregious, sharing a genuine sense of humility can go a long way. When stories go sideways, emotion will almost always trump reason, and your business will only make matters worse if you blame the circumstance on some other factor instead of accepting responsibility.

As shared earlier, your audience is watching you intently, including how you present yourself along with your personal presentation, which I covered in Chapter 6, "People power". For example, if your story that went sideways includes being directly or indirectly responsible for an environmental disaster (hopefully not!), showing up in a three-piece suit or power suit at the response location will juxtapose dramatically against those on the scene who are most likely dirty or dishevelled.

Timeliness

If your business is directly tied to or responsible for an event or circumstance that sends the story of your business sideways, if you don't respond in a timely manner (when required), I can guarantee you that someone else will, either online with social media and/ or with the mainstream media. If indirectly affected by the event or circumstance, you can buy yourself more time, depending on how impactful that circumstance is on your business. In Erick's situation, the amount of negative discourse about his comments were growing rapidly online by the hour, which made connecting with his stakeholders even more important in a timely manner, executing his company's response plan shortly after the event that caused his story to go sideways.

In other scenarios, like a major event, in absence of information, people will be left to their own devices, and I mean that both literally and figuratively. Remember, when your story goes sideways, you're also trying to not make it worse, but managing the paradox of proximity: respond in a timely manner, but don't rush something to your own media network or the mainstream media that will make matters worse. A common practice to bide your business some time is to draft holding statements that indicate you've identified the issue and will have more information shortly. Sometimes – most times – it is better to take a few more punches from media and the online commentariat than risk creating greater damage to your company's reputation.

Technology

The fourth "T" of taking control is technology. In the early stages of taking control, staying top of misinformation or errors that pop up on social media is crucial. As part of the team you designate to manage matters, assign someone specifically to monitor your social media feeds and external feeds of key media in your market. Correct misinformation when it's incorrect and perpetuates a negative narrative based on inaccuracy. Avoid responding to any commentary online that's outside of correcting inaccurate information about the circumstance such as opinions, which as hard as it may be to stomach, you may be drawn into an online debate that you simply cannot win in the moment, recalling that emotion trumps reason when stories go sideways.

The irony of having your own media network is that it can also be one of your greatest sources of losing control of the very story you're wanting to share, while at the same time, be your greatest source of distributing your story widely. Keep in mind, "When stories go sideways" is a chapter based on some of the worst-case scenarios to guide you in the event you find your business in a sideways situation. An effective resource to help you monitor commentary online, whether your story is sideways or not, is to consider social listening and media monitoring programs found online with a simple search in your favourite web browser. Some of these programs require various levels of investment not only in money but the time to learn how to use them. Depending on the quantity and profile of your storytelling plans, it's always worthwhile to explore the benefits of these platforms, which even at the exploratory level, show you what their platforms monitor to keep businesses like yours in the loop. I've led communications for large organizations and prominent clients with multiple business interests, making it challenging to keep on top of everything with a negative sentiment posted online; the same goes for missing the opportunity to see positive coverage. Furthermore, these kinds of platforms, when initialized, provide up-to-the-minute reporting when timing, as we know, is of the essence. For example, late one evening, with the social listening platform's app installed on my smartphone, I had a series of alerts tracking an open letter criticizing one of my client's companies and her personally as a leader. Related, that same leader was scheduled to speak at a high-profile engagement early the next morning, with a heavy presence of media. Thankfully, getting the warning in advance allowed me to get in front of the issue with my client, preparing her for the inevitable questions from the media about the emerging matter online. Additionally, some platforms offer sophisticated features such as measuring the sentiment of posts in the categories of negative, positive, or neutral, which make for insightful data whether your story is sideways or not.

If you're a small business with a smaller budget, investing in online third-party platforms may be beyond your reach and expertise, but that doesn't mean you're flying blind online. Most of the leading search engines give you the ability to create alerts on anything related to the key words you assign for monitoring, and as it relates to your business, that would include any key brand names, leaders, products, or services. Again, for the context of this chapter, setting up search engine alerts assists you in tracking negative references about the story of your business, but also captures positive references, too.

Internal communications

In the next chapter, "The inside story", I designate a full chapter to internal communications. What's expressed externally about your business when your story goes sideways is also shared internally, as your internal stakeholders consume content with the same channels of communication you deploy to tell the story of your business. The importance of internal stakeholders cannot be overstated, and this is why developing your response strategy to a sideways story for this priority audience should not be taken for granted, which many companies do, expecting "loyal employees" to not believe everything they're reading and seeing externally. As you may recall in the chapter's case study, Erick made communicating to his employees a top priority to ensure they were in the loop and their feelings were acknowledged and managed. Just like your external stakeholders, in absence of information from you, your internal audience will fill the information gap on their own with whatever is at their disposal.

The power of your people

Reinforcing what we learned in Chapter 6's "People power", we circle back on what is your company's best asset when telling or defending the story of your business if your story goes sideways. As the old axiom goes, fail to plan, then plan to fail, and never have truer words been said when it comes to creating a plan if your story goes sideways.

Create crisis comms team

Let's be honest, no one ever wants to think about what happens if your story goes sideways. But I'd respectfully suggest that if you're going to embark on the storytelling journey for your business, that you haven't truly thought it through unless your business, at the very minimum, considers the negative outcomes of posting content externally. One of the best ways to plan in advance is to establish your team.

Understanding not all businesses are created the same when it comes to the professionals they employ, I'll start with some of the key people you need on your team, leaving it up to you to consider if you have what you need or whether you need to secure some resources from a third-party service, most of which we've covered in the preceding chapters.

Communications professionals generally have the experience, training, and greatest understanding of the external landscape (mainstream and social media) and make optimal point people to develop and execute strategies when stories go sideways. If you don't have dedicated communications or public relations support, designating someone with competent writing skills, both formal and informal, will serve your business well in a sideways story situation. Supporting team members must include the leader of the business or someone near the top that has the authority to make decisions on behalf of the organization. Including your operations lead provides the technical information required if operations or facilities are affected because of a story going sideways.

Administrative and support leads including legal provide immediate access to guidance and direction to manage sensitive language and its interpretation in response to accountability requests from the media by way of example. A human resources leader provides insight on how responses externally will be perceived internally and how to communicate directly to internal stakeholders.

If you're posting and distributing your stories externally on your own media network, then you have designated a social media lead or you have invested in external social support. When assessing if these people have the social media skills and experience to tell your story, take the time to also assess that they have the tools and ability to defend your story when necessary.

Identify and train spokespeople

As part of building your crisis communications team when a story goes sideways, assessing and assigning the right spokespeople will ultimately determine how your plan and responses will be delivered and then received by your stakeholders if speaking directly to your audience is necessary. Depending on the severity of the issue, your spokesperson can cover the range of your people within your company from senior leadership to product or service specialist. Obviously, in the most severe circumstances, the most senior leadership is highly advisable, but not always. During the COVID-19 pandemic, public health officers and epidemiologists were often the key spokespeople governments leaned on to build trust with a confused and, at times, very suspicious public, struggling to learn about a virus that suspended their lives for a significant amount of time. Generally, the bigger the issue you have to manage, requiring your spokesperson to be front facing in the public, the higher up the seniority level you'll need to pull from your organization.

Worth the risk

One of the biggest fears of any spokesperson or the senior storyteller who grooms them is that an interview or interaction with the media is going to go sideways. I wish I could say otherwise, but every once in a while, a sideways scenario will occur. I debated even adding this section to this chapter, but wanted to extoll the benefit of my experience watching other storytellers get caught up in controversy when interacting with media and social media. Restating, of the thousands of stories I have been involved with only a small percentage have required a range of tactful communications to get the story back on track. The immense value and benefit of storytelling overwhelmingly outweighs the risk of a story going sideways, but it can happen, and if you're going to share the story of your business externally, without hesitation, I can assure you it is absolutely worth the risk. Increasing the odds in your favour to swerve a story going sideways means embracing the tools and techniques throughout *Storytelling for Business*.

Recruit Touchstone Team

Telling the story of your business is deeply personal as well as professional. As a result, that connection leads to some compelling storytelling elements, but it can also lead to becoming too close to the story if it goes sideways, leaving the most experienced storyteller unable to react and respond objectively. Creating a Touchstone Team, consisting of two to three people who preferably don't work for you or are not directly invested in your organization, but are equally proud champions of your business, can guide you to see the forest through the proverbial trees when your business is being held to account when a story goes sideways. Yes, they have self-interest in your company, but have a level or two of detachment from not owning or working for the company, and as a result, serve as superior sounding boards, offering timely, knowledgeable, and trustworthy advice when your business really needs it most. A touchstone, for your reference, is anecdotally known as a measurement of merit for which ideas and concepts can be tested. Adding a team of trusted advisors as your touchstone is my basis for recommending a Touchstone Team, and when stories go intensely sideways, this team can prove invaluable as another perspective when sometimes one is desperately needed.

Build it up to tear it down

In one of their best-selling books called *Decisive*, authors and brothers Chip and Dan Heath say one of the biggest mistakes people make when making decisions is being overconfident.[1] To mitigate regretful decisions that cost time, money, and resources, the Heaths present a number of strategies to see your ideas as failures before you are making a big decision. Accordingly, investing in storytelling for business should be considered a big decision for your company. As part of your story telling planning, consider the Heath brothers' "premortem", looking at your story a year from now to see how it failed to achieve its objectives, and then assess how you can pivot on those storytelling shortcomings.

Further to the Heath brothers' premortem strategy, I have found other traditional models very helpful for creating business storytelling campaigns. Power mapping provides an easy-to-reference model, where you can plot out who will potentially influence what you're trying to do in your story or identify those who may act as detractors. I covered a number of stakeholders earlier in this chapter for your storytelling consideration. And, while traditionally a business or marketing assessment model, SWOT analysis works quite well as part of your storytelling planning. SWOT stands for strengths, weaknesses, opportunities, and threats, and is a proven model to assess your risks and rewards both internally and externally.

By way of example, strengths and weaknesses are external. For Erick's event, a strength was he had earned a great deal of public trust with people externally that matter the most to his business, including customers. A weakness identified for Erick was special interest groups who would leverage his company's profile to increase awareness of their cause or issue. Would these groups show up at the event? Numerous scenarios were presented and thought out if they did.

Opportunities and threats are internal. Erick's company had developed significant trust with their employees, and anticipated they'd be champions of the news both through the grapevine and on their social media. However, like all SWOT categories, what poses an opportunity internally can also be a threat externally. Erick and his team benefited from a strong internal company culture, but they knew not everyone was happy, and assessed any negative internal messaging that might be shared or event plans that could've been leaked to the media in-advance.

Target on your back

Despite their very best efforts, some businesses and organizations simply will have targets on their backs, and a variety of external entities are aiming for them to further their agendas as shared in Chapter 7, "Audience analysis". For example, one influencer who made it his mandate to advocate less government subsidies for private interest would put my client's business in his crosshairs and fire away. Even though there were literally hundreds of other businesses that secured government grants legitimately that this influencer could have targeted, he chose my client because they are a very high-profile organization and targeting them would lead to some temporary traction online, and in a few instances, catching the attention of the mainstream media. That was exactly what the influencer had in mind. For what it's worth, it's a short-lived tactic by the influencer as the media are savvy too, and don't like to be used excessively as a service to prop up an agenda.

Furthermore, when a story goes sideways, some people or other external entities will never be satisfied, no matter what you do to genuinely resolve the situation. That may be cold comfort, but warm up as you can't fool the public, and experience has demonstrated that if you genuinely do what's right, the public will support you, and the detractors that hold on eventually burn themselves out as no one is paying attention any longer or they simply fade away.

Sometimes it's okay to stay silent

One of the questions I get asked most often is does my business have to respond to the media or an unfavourable comment on social media? Well, that depends, sometimes "yes" and sometimes "no". This chapter has mainly focused on "yes", and for some perspective, I feel beholden to share some rationale for "no". To gauge your response or lack thereof, how does it compare to the severity of the issue that needs to be managed? If it's a social media post that garnered a tepid response from the online commentariat, you risk making matters worse if you engage on a negative comment or response based on opinion, especially if others are trying to leverage the negative story to their advantage, and that can, and will happen. As for the media, depending on the intensity of what your business is being held to account for, there are times where you can assess that not saying anything will cause less reputational harm than giving the media a story that will no longer be a story the next day. Making these assessments is rarely done well in isolation, and that's why you have invested the time and effort to create a crisis communications team and your Touchstone Team.

After the storm has passed

The one predictability about weather is that it's always unpredictable. To borrow the analogy, once the storm of a sideways story has passed, it's inevitable that another one could be on the horizon, but most likely not for some time. As you know from running your business, some of the best opportunities to learn and get better at what you do come from when you have a setback in business. And the same goes for when your story goes sideways. Within proximity to the event or circumstance that caused your story to go sideways, bring your teams and others who can objectively provide valuable feedback from the experience to see how your plan worked or could have been better, setting you up for greater success in the future. Furthermore, take the time to evaluate with all aspects of your business for feedback. Often some very good suggestions come from other stakeholders who see a way to make things even better. Over time, there have been many case studies that have documented businesses that not only survived when their story went sideways, but also thrived, having created better products and services that were exposed as insufficient, and in the process created stronger relationships with all their stakeholders.

Worth repeating

Case study: When a story goes sideways

- Understand that despite best intentions and planning, your business story can inadvertently become controversial
- Know that even when a story goes sideways, your business can survive and even thrive after the negative publicity subsides

Things don't always go as planned

- Accept that the unexpected can happen, and when it does, embrace the four T's of taking control of your story gone sideways:
  - Transparency
  - Trustworthiness
  - Timeliness
  - Technology

Internal communications

- Remember what you share externally is consumed internally by your employees, suppliers, and other important stakeholders
- Keep internal audiences top of mind as well when managing an external issue

The power of your people

Turn to your (internal) people when a story goes sideways:

- Create crisis comms team
- Identify and train spokespeople
- Worth the risk
- Recruit Touchstone Team
- Build it up to tear it down

Target on your back

- Accept that even with all the planning and mitigation possible, you and your business may still have a target on your back
- Understand that sometimes it's okay to stay silent

After the storm has passed

- Take the opportunity to review the events surrounding your sideways story while it's still fresh
- Include your Touchstone Team

9
The inside story

Case study: The inside story on storytelling

Over the past 20 years, Andie and Dev have created a contemporary, inclusive, and inspirational health and wellness business that has become tremendously successful. For simplicity, I'll refer to their business as Deven's (not real name) and they've become a textbook case study for building their own media network, which has facilitated the company's consistent and steady growth. Understanding the power of people (see Chapter 6, "People power"), owners Andie and Dev star in most of the company's videos to tell the stories of their business, including showing real-world utility for their products and services. The commitment to their own media network has galvanized their followers, which has grown into the tens of thousands on their main social media platforms and kept them running profitable during difficult times like the COVID pandemic that forced them to close their studios temporarily.

As popular as Andie and Dev are among their fervent client base, they've built their health and wellness "empire" by recognizing, empowering, and investing in their most important stakeholders – their employees. Understanding that their employees live their well-being values into what Andie and Dev call a "working lifestyle", they decided to channel their employees' immense outreach to grow a movement larger than the business itself – a relentless pursuit of well-being in every aspect of life. And, through that narrative pursuit of well-being, Deven's products and services were authentically woven into stories as a means to embracing health and wellness at almost every opportunity.

Deven's own media network of social media, content development, publicity, and community relations does not come cheap for Andie and Dev, who commit a significant portion of their operating budget to internal and external storytellers, along with the upkeep of the equipment, software, training, and other tools. As part of their storytelling strategy is a commitment to measuring if their content is resonating with their customers and other important audiences, I'll go into greater detail about storytelling measurement in the next chapter.

A few of Deven's long-time staffers can be considered influencers in their own right (see Chapter 7, "Audience analysis"), with thousands of loyal followers of their own. As covered throughout *Storytelling for Business*, Andie and Dev know that the showcasing of "real people" produces far greater engagement compared to the company or organization they're associated with. That's not to suggest when harnessing the reach of your internal stakeholders you let them run wild with absolutely no checks and balances with your products and services, but with proper storytelling planning, an inside story will yield you as much (or sometimes more) engagement with your business than an externally focused story.

Dev decided to lean into his staffers' penchant for posting about their working lifestyle experiences that include working with clients, using products, or in some cases, show how services worked in live, real-time. As part of Andie and Dev's measurement strategy, they used surveys to confirm if their employees' storytelling was working, and every quarterly survey indicated it was in a tangible way.

Andie and Dev recognized that to keep this mutually beneficial storytelling strategy sustainable, they needed to include their employees in developing the content calendar for Deven's own media network. When sales targets were reached through increased sales as a result of Deven's media network, along with their employees' media networks, they agree in-advance on incentives, such as a percentage of sales going to a charity or community initiatives.

For Andie and Dev, the inside story of their storytelling success means involving their employees at every level of business storytelling development and creating an environment of trust to share stories outside of Dev's own media network. His business has learned to expand its storytelling capacity through its employees, and I'll give you the inside story on how you can do the same with your internal stakeholders.

A look ahead

In Chapter 9, we look inward to tell the story of your business from an internal perspective. Your internal stakeholders, especially your employees, are the most powerful storytellers within your network. In the case study, Dev was impressed with the engagement his employees were getting on social media, especially when they shared their excitement and passion for his company's products and services. With a plan to communicate the expectations and reward the results, Dev harnessed the power of his most valuable storytelling asset – his people. In Chapter 9, we'll explore how to identify your most valuable assets and how to empower them to become your organization's ultimate ambassadors.

The growth of internal storytelling

As shared early on in *Storytelling for Business*, telling stories is one of the most effective methods to influence your stakeholders to take action or accept change, and this premise is underscored with internal stakeholders such as employees, volunteers, and other enablers. Oxytocin is the "feel good" chemical produced in the body that allows our minds to connect with and understand emotions that evoke change and facilitate influence, and that is why many companies have invested in developing capacity for internal storytelling as independent business units to lead communications with an organization. By employing storytelling as a primary communications tool for internal audiences, many businesses have found great success sharing larger and often complex policies, sales strategies, or business operations, which become easier to ascertain and adopt when shared through the power of storytelling.

In my observations of the communications industry over the years, especially in the past decade, no segment of business storytelling has grown more in its influence and impact within organizations than with internal communications. For example, many larger companies I have worked with that have measured and recognized the considerable value of internal storytelling and communications sometimes split their communications into two teams – internal and external, led by professionals with titles such as vice-president, internal communications. If you're looking for the inside story on why internal storytelling continues to get results with internal stakeholders, I cover some of the main reasons in the following section.

Uniting a growing remote workforce

Technology has allowed companies to spread more of their employees across different locations, not to mention across time zones, and even across countries. And therein lies another paradox of technology: it brings us altogether but at the same time leads to greater separation. Many companies experienced this situation during the COVID-19 pandemic, forcing millions of people to work remotely, and the same time disconnecting from their daily workplace routines, and all the cultural benefits companies invest heavily in to keep their employees connected. Whatever the circumstance, whether it's something as dramatic as a pandemic or an oil and gas company with hundreds of employees spread out across dozens of remote locations, business communicators rely on storytelling through the internal and external channels of communication to keep their most important stakeholder group engaged.

Strengthening company's culture

As mentioned, one of the most recognizable benefits of internal storytelling for business is strengthening a company's culture among its staff. A strong culture is what created the opportunity in the first place for Dev to see such enormous potential for grooming his employees as ultimate company storytellers and ambassadors, and he made sure to include and reward them. Many companies build their recruitment and retention strategy around company storytelling.

Tapping into your own media network, some of the tactics to tell internal stories range from employee profiles celebrating success to leaders starting all-hands meetings with challenges raised or shared directly by employees. Organizations with more developed storytelling capacity repurpose their stories from internal tools, covered in greater detail later in this chapter, to external tools, all with the strategic intent of recognizing, developing, celebrating, and ultimately strengthening company culture.

Revisiting for the benefit of reinforcement, at the centre of any remarkable story are real people, and while leaders certainly have their place in storytelling, consider showcasing the successes and challenges of "everyday" employees through their stories. People connect to business ideas and concepts and learn how to incorporate them into their work if they can easily relate to others, and what better way than through people just like them? Working with leaders to share big news internally, I suggest including staff from all levels of their business to tell the story, taking lead roles such as co-hosting/hosting townhalls, or less high-profile approaches, but equally impactful, such as appearing in company collateral material or training videos. Just remember to invest the time and energy to the tools and tactics we covered in Chapter 6, "People power", setting your employees up for storytelling success.

Keeping calm during crisis

One of the most important reasons to invest in your business storytelling capacity comes during times of crisis or great challenge. When crisis strikes, your most important stakeholder group becomes immediately evident as they need to be relied on to maintain operations or shut them down (if necessary), or act as ambassadors among their peers in their community as sources of information. Developing your internal storytelling network will allow your business to connect quickly and efficiently when information is usually at its most sensitive and not immediately understood, for example during a situation that is beyond your company's control such as a disaster or tragedy. Even externally, you may recall how in these very intense situations, one of the first stories leaders often tell is about their family of employees, empathizing and reaching out to them.

In circumstances where difficult stories need to be told – even when these are planned, such as layoffs or organizational downsizing and restructuring – having a trusted internal storytelling strategy may not make the delivery any easier, but it certainly allows your business to deliver tough stories accurately and respectfully.

Creating constructive conversation

Internal business storytelling creates constructive conversations, opening meaningful two-way conversations that lead to innovation and ideas to resolving conflict and controversy. The key is genuinely being open to not only developing tools to encourage the sharing of internal stories, but following through to accept them, and share them through your internal channel of communication. Many companies I have worked with enjoyed constructive conversations with their internal stakeholders through technology, including intranets or apps, to tried and true all-hands meetings or the basic drop box for suggestions. Again, what anchors their internal storytelling strategy is trust in the tools and the people who put them in place to tell their stories.

Identifying and understanding internal stakeholders

For many companies, their staff is their priority stakeholder group, but it's important to remember that they're not the only internal stakeholder group to be considered. When developing your internal storytelling strategy, think about what other internal stakeholder groups have a stake in the ongoing success of your company. Some of the other internal stakeholder group include suppliers, vendors, board members, consultants, and lenders, just to name a few. For non-profits, additional internal stakeholders include volunteers and donors, among others. The point with this list of internal audiences is to get you thinking about them and how they influence the success of your business. For Dev, he'd make a point of sharing his content directly to his suppliers and lenders, often including direct and indirect positive references to their brands, seeking permission first when necessary. Internal stakeholders have more influence than you may realize, and it is certainly worth building them into your internal storytelling strategy where possible. While not directly tied to your business like your employees, other internal audiences remain indirectly connected, interacting with your staff and customers daily and through many different touch points throughout your business. Keep them in mind, how to communicate with them through your own media network and their channels of communication. Your success is their success, and they're also paying close attention to your challenges.

Leading leaders

If you're the leader of your business or you're in charge of your leader's internal storytelling strategy, I'll share some of the storytelling aspects I've had business leaders successfully incorporate into their narratives to build trust, connect with the people internally who matter most, and drive storytelling impact.

Start with a story

As this is *Storytelling for Business*, it should come as no surprise that I advocate for starting with a story, especially when the content can be challenging or technical. For example, when introducing a new company-wide policy, start with a story, either directly or non-directly related. Some leaders may choose to draw on their past professional experience or even personal experience as a parent or something relatable from their youth. Related, I will either advise a business to take an informal or informal survey following a leader's presentation to see and hear what content most resonated, and more often than not, it was the sharing of a story that connected the content to something that was relatable to all.

Increase visibility

Your business may be like many others – spread across numerous floors, buildings, or other cities and countries. Where possible, in making your visits, make a concerted effort to be seen, even if it's briefly walking through locations you don't normally get the opportunity to visit. Along the way, share your presence to maximize your time and effort. One of my clients had store locations in cities spread out across eastern Canada, and he posted selfie images to the company's social media app where he appeared standing in front of company landmarks or with groups of employees he rarely gets to see. As you can imagine, his presence was amplified through his company's channel of communication, increasing his visibility. Many a successful politician has done the same over the years from bus tours to selfie promotion as they tour the regions within their constituency, again, to raise their visibility, and just as importantly, increase the appearance of their visibility.

Express vulnerability

When I start to work with a leader to tell their story internally, they share this self-imposed pressure to always project that they are always in control or have all the answers. In the majority of stories your business will tell, and as I've covered in numerous points through *Storytelling for Business*, it is more than okay to not know all the answers and to express vulnerability. By letting your guard down, you create a safety in a "we're all in this together" scenario, developing an environment that leads to greater collaboration, more innovation, and increase of problem-solving, again insights gleaned from post-presentation/storytelling initiatives. Your employees and other internal stakeholders are certainly looking to you to project confidence and leadership and including a personal approach through vulnerability can also go a long way to having your story resonate.

Express gratitude

I once worked with a client who owned and operated a very large manufacturing plant with many departments undertaking diverse forms of work. Some of the skills required special trades, along with the stamina to complete work that was physically demanding. Genuinely striving to be visible to all his employees was important to this leader, and so was expressing gratitude. He developed a storytelling campaign where he job-shadowed a variety of employees. He allowed himself to be vulnerable, coming across as inexperienced at the task at hand, which was the entire point. He can't do everything and needs all his employees to operate the company. The thrust of the story series was to express gratitude by his ability to be visible and vulnerable. The story series has become very popular on the company's internal channels of communication, and cultural topics of discussion around the water cooler and lunchrooms. As always, gathering feedback to become better storytellers, what connected most with employees about the job-shadowing content was their leader's authentic expression of gratitude for all contribution from his employees.

Internal tools and technology

As shared in Chapter 8, the fourth "T" in taking control of a sideways story is technology, and it's just as prominent in a proactive internal storytelling strategy as it is in a reactive story gone sideways. Of the top ten communication tools used by business communicators, the top two are done using the internet – email (#1) and intranet (#2) – and among the most popular social media platforms used for employee engagement are Facebook, instant messaging, Twitter, and blogs according to a study commissioned by the International Association of Business Communicators (IABC).[1] Though as social media platforms ebb and flow in popularity, or simply come and go, the top tools your business uses to tell your stories internally will, I suspect, differ from the stats cited above.

Whether or not you choose to invest in technology to tell the story of your business, what's known for sure is that your employees and internal stakeholders are online and active, and in many cases sharing their stories about your business.

Here are some of the commonly used communication tools to assist in telling your business story using the internal segments of the SWOT analysis shared in the previous chapter:

Internal media network	Opportunities	Threats
Email	Still one of the most effective channels of internal communication as messages are delivered right to employees' primary channel of communication	Email fatigue dilutes potency of messaging Younger demographics turning away from email
Email newsletters	Delivered directly into employees' inboxes and provide insightful data (see next chapter)	Managing third-party platforms can be time-consuming and expensive
	Remain preferred channel of communication for storytelling and company information	Don't always show proper formatting (images deleted) End up in junk folders, until manually instructed otherwise
	Third-party programs can integrate into mainstream email programs	

Company website	A source of storytelling pride as the website is external to the public and accessible to employees	Primarily external, therefore many internal and cultural details and nuances are left out
Intranet	A centre point for documentation and policies, calendars, admin Use home page as a story	Generally doesn't integrate well with company's standard communications tools (email, website, etc.) Create competition for other tools (e-newsletters, magazines)
Videos (live/ virtual)	Growing rapidly in popularity and necessity with a dramatic increase in remote workforces Plethora of online third-party platforms that are easy to use and integrate well with standard content production tools	Greater risk of hacking from uninvited guests Security protocols, while good and getting better, are still outside of the company
Videos (produced)	Great content that can be repurposed internally and externally Good format for training purposes One of the most effective ways to tell a story for internal stakeholders, working with ideas or policies that require a "show and tell" approach	Has a shelf life and gets outdated If not monitored, post video content can become an archive of stories that may no longer align with your company's values

Social media (internal)	Mainstream apps reconfigured specifically for internal usage; familiarity of mainstream social media makes it easier for employees to learn and adopt Companies that pay for cell phone plans can make installation and use of internal apps mandatory or recommended	Notifications can be perceived as pushy or intrusive Third-party apps are expensive Of all the channels of internal storytelling, employee apps remain one of the most resisted and hardest to achieve buy-in
Social media (external)	Most commonly used among younger demographics; initialized on most mobile phones; create power opportunities to share and promote company messages organic showcase of company culture	Proceed with caution (see "Social media policy" in this chapter)
Instant messaging	Available on all mobile phones Available as part of social media apps and third-party apps Companies that pay for cell phone plans can make installation and use of messaging mandatory or recommended	Outside of a company's control and security network Lose control of ability to distribute communications Lose ability to collect backend data A never-ending supply of instant messaging options, diluting the opportunity to establish a clear choice for your business

Company magazine or printed newsletter or report	Online platforms now exist where you can retain the high-quality of print production while viewing online An online search of "online magazine platform" will yield some great options to consider Viable option for repurposed content; ideal platform for annual reports Transferable to online magazine platforms	Out of step with sustainability initiatives, if printed Internal stakeholders spending less time reading, and the hours invested in producing this long-form content may not be worth the return on readership
Posters	Good resource for lunchrooms and washrooms and other areas of high traffic	Get outdated quickly, and if no one is monitoring the message boards, the posters pile up on top of each other
Townhall/ all-hands meetings	Good for big announcements at physical location Great for culture building With virtual capabilities, townhall meetings can reach more people in less time, across multiple locations Recordings ensure everyone gets a chance to see the big event	Time-consuming to produce Difficult to get everyone in all the same place at the same time Virtual options pose a greater risk of being shared, in whole or in part (via recording), outside of the company

Visual media (LED screens)	LED screens range in size from 5+ feet to just inches, making them accessible in all types of locations	If connected by a media network, the cost to set up, program, and maintain is expensive
	If the screens are attached to a network, they are easy to update from one source	If off-networks, the content becomes outdated quickly as it's not as accessible as a network
		The hardware and software needs regular maintenance and replacement

Mix your media

One of the biggest challenges when telling the story of your business internally is navigating a diverse group of internal stakeholders. In Chapter 7, "Audience analysis", recall the need of getting graphic, understanding the differences between demographics, psychographics, and geographics. Internally, demographics, for example, can mean what a 20-year-old employee relies on for company storytelling can contrast remarkably to that of a 50-year-old employee. When building your own media network internally, remember that while email remains one of the most popular methods to tell your story, it's not the most popular or preferred method to receive stories. Data may show a 50-year-old staffer will engage with your stories via email platforms, but that a 20-year-old staffer will most likely choose to engage with something more mobile, like an instant message social platform or the messaging service associated with their mobile phone. Much like your external media network, build your internal storytelling capacity by investing strategically in a mix of media, which also assists with managing the forced rank most businesses find themselves managing. Depending your company's leadership, the ones at the top usually determine, based on their preference, how and where your stories are consumed, and as many top executives still rarely use social media for fear of breaching company policies or looking foolish themselves, this scenario can stifle the advent of contemporary communications. As a result, many companies default to the tried-and-true channels of communication. That's not necessarily a criticism, but the point worth raising is to identify your priorities for storytelling within your business and that the channels you think you've identified to tell your story may not necessarily be the most ideal.

Is your company culture committed?

Before building your internal media network to tell your story, invest in understanding if some channels are beyond the comfort level of your company's culture. For example, some organizations make a concerted effort to celebrate success, both as a company, as teams within the company, and as individuals, such as employees. If this is your company culture, then internal social media applications, both for internal and external use, will be a good fit as telling the success story is a fit with your company's culture. Conversely, if your company's culture is reserved and takes a more private approach to success storytelling, using tools that amplify those stories in a pronounced way, will create a counterculture for sharing stories internally. Whether it's a cool employee app or innovative intranet add-on, just because it's available to you, doesn't necessarily mean it's a fit for your company's culture. Knowing your company's culture for communication and storytelling before you begin to develop your internal storytelling strategy or produce any campaign is essential. Many businesses that invest time, energy, and resources into new platforms fail because they don't invest a proportionate amount of time, energy, and resources to see and hear whether their internal stakeholders would use or embrace them.

Social media policy

Next to developing a crisis communication plan for when stories go sideways, the plan I find most often avoided for managing business stories is a social media policy for internal stakeholders. In fact, according to the comprehensive IABC study referred to earlier in this chapter, one third of companies surveyed don't have a social media policy for their employees.[2] As shared at many checkpoints throughout *Storytelling for Business*, creating and maintaining your own media network is unique to your business, and with so many options to begin with, developing a social media plan to govern it can seem like a daunting task. I suggest it doesn't need to be if you let common sense guide your social media channels within your own media network. For example, simply providing a policy of inclusiveness with your employees like Dev did, allows for the sharing of ideas and responsibilities to tell stories, while managing any associated risks as they're identified with a collaborative approach. Social media plans for companies can vary to suit the culture of the business and the preferred channels of communications for internal and external stakeholders, but generally, the following will guide you in developing your social media plan.

Empower people power

The most proficient social media policies are the ones that put the onus and accountability on the internal stakeholders who administer and populate the social media channels with content, which is most notably your employees, but in some cases, that can also mean an external third-party service provider. The larger a business becomes with its own media network, generally the more social platforms it uses for internal and external storytelling. The pitfall for companies that grow with too many platforms, too soon is they lose track of who's doing what and when, and that can lead to duplicate platforms with many users. And, if any of them leave your business without the right checks and balances, their legacy accounts can linger online with outdated content. To mitigate the pitfall of platforms, create a record of who's using what platforms, and make sure this record is well-known to leaders and those who tell your stories.

Using your favourite search engine, look up social media aggregators for a variety of platforms designed specifically to manage all your social media platforms, not only for security, but for the ability to post and share content at the same time. As part of your social media plan, review all the above annually, at a minimum. Social media platforms come and go, and the leading platforms change often with updates throughout the year. And, most importantly, review the list of employees managing accounts, removing departed managers as needed. As obvious as this may seem, as part of your social media management policy, remind your employees to double, even triple check, that before they post on their private accounts they make sure they're not posting from the company's social media.

Most of the major social accounts allow users to have multiple accounts on the same platform. The inherit danger in that setup is it can be easy to think you're on your personal account, when sometimes you're posting from the company's account if you're the administrator of that account. It can and does happen, and a simple search engine reveal will show some mainly humorous, but ultimately embarrassing (to both the company and user), posts that can be corrected with a quick retraction. As per the chapter's case study, as Dev was aware that one of his best "internal social influencers" was also the employee in charge of his company's lead social channels, he communicated the safeguard of proper account login policies on a regular, but respectful, basis.

Externally, communicate the differentiation between company and personal accounts. Company accounts generally have some part of the company's name and are owned by the organization itself. Personal accounts are owned by your employees and are their property. Depending on your company's culture for sharing and storytelling, as discussed earlier, set clear expectations on how your employees communicate your business when online. Either way, some of your employees are sharing their experiences about your business online, and when their stories go sideways, it's usually because of the absence of a social media plan with clear and collaborative policies.

Communicate clarity

Clarity is kindness. Therefore, be kind to your internal stakeholders by communicating with clarity what goes on and what stays off your company's social media platforms. Again, common sense rules in that staying away from any derogatory or negative language is paramount, and any content shared on your company's channels should be anchored in service, insightfulness, and enlightenment. The people who consume your stories via your social posts should be better off for the experience, not worse.

Remember, you don't own or control your employees' social media platforms, and most social media policies recommend that personal accounts share the disclaimer that opinions expressed are that of the individual, and not the company.

If your company's culture is to leverage your employees' collective reach, like Dev's does, do so with a smart and strategic approach. For example, if you empower your employees to assist in spreading the word about a product or service, asking them to come up with their own posts may lead to unexpected and unfavourable results; instead creating posts on your own channels with the suggestion to simply "endorse" with a like or share will come across as more organic and authentic, and relieve unnecessary pressure for your employees. This kind of collaborative approach is at the core of Dev's successful social media strategy with his employees. Everyone buys in to the policies because they all had a hand in creating them.

The social media universe lives and breathes 24/7, and so should your social media policy, even during off hours. Clearly communicate that your company's policy needs to be considered when posting anything about the company at all times, even after hours.

Set the tone

How does your company want to tell its story internally and externally? Think about some of your favourite corporate social media channels. What is it about them that keeps you coming back for more content or engaging with them on a regular basis? For example, some very large corporations, like major airlines or government agencies, have a sassy and fun tone to their language, responding publicly to people who complain about them, sometimes with self-deprecating humour or by turning the tables, respectfully, on when someone clearly has failed to read the fine print. That may not be the tone for your company, and that's fine, but a consistent voice needs to be determined across all your platforms to ensure your stakeholders understand the tone and message that you want to convey. For Dev and his team, they want to portray a healthy lifestyle where the company's products and services complement well-being and mental wellness. That ethos is then shared in their storytelling.

Where many businesses get themselves in trouble with social media is pretending to be someone they're not, attempting to pass themselves off as personal accounts of individuals advocating a little too much in favour of everything the company's doing. Remember, you can't fool the public, and even the most basic social media user can root out rhetoric that's not authentic.

Social in style

I remember one communications department I was leading spending literally hours debating the "proper" use of the comma with my direct reports, which is a never-ending debate for countless storytellers and business communicators. While I always appreciate a healthy debate about discourse and rhetoric, clearly this was not the best use of my time or my team's. Remembering clarity is kindness, we embarked on the journey to create a style guide for the company. A style guide essentially guides your organization on how exactly to say or spell specific words, definitions, and phrases, unique to your corporate lexicon, which includes the proper use of pronouns and phrases that are respectful of diversity and inclusion initiatives. Additionally, style guides are tremendous resources for your employees looking for a uniform approach to social media posts and hashtags. The typical corporate style guides base themselves off an industry standard style guide like the American Press or Canadian Press style guides or a number of leading academic style guides. And, when it comes to correct spelling for definitions, choose a reputable dictionary, and the version that's drafted for your country. For example, in Canada, where I live, the style guides I've written are based off the Canadian Press style guide and the Canadian edition of the Oxford Dictionary.

Worth repeating

Case study: The inside story on storytelling

- Explore internal stakeholders (employees) as storytellers of your business
- Include internal audiences in your storytelling planning, production, and distribution processes
- Provide clear direction and expectations

The growth of internal storytelling

- Uniting a growing remote workforce
- Strengthening company's culture
- Keeping calm during crisis
- Creating constructive conversation

Identifying and understanding internal stakeholders

- Identify and inform all internal stakeholders about storytelling (suppliers, for example)
- Repurpose your content to engage all internal audiences

Leading leaders

- Start with a story
- Increase visibility
- Express vulnerability
- Express gratitude

Internal tools and technology

- Understand your employees and internal stakeholders are online and active, sharing their stories about your business, whether you choose to acknowledge them or not
- Provide your employees the right tools and technology to facilitate internal storytelling and the ability to guide and monitor the process, both to enhance and strengthen internal culture

Mix your media

- Use a variety of media to reach your internal audiences, not relying on just one medium

Is your company culture committed?

- Determine what the comfort level is of your internal stakeholders to participate in and/or share storytelling content

Social media policy

- Empower your internal audiences to tell their stories, but guide them with a plan
- Communicate with clarity what goes on and what stays off your company's social media platforms
- Set the tone for how you want your business to be perceived online – are you serious or light-hearted?

Social in style

- Create a uniform style of language via a style guide

10

Making measurement matter

Case study: Building a case for measurement

Recruiting well-trained and experienced professionals in the culinary field has become increasingly difficult in the hospitality industry, desperate for chefs and supporting staff as competing industries were enticing people into their professions more strategically and assertively. Art was hearing almost daily from the hundreds of members who belonged to the hospitality association he led, which he has served as the venerable executive director for the past 26 years. At the root of the problem was a dearth of new talent, specifically younger people, getting into the culinary trade.

To their distinct advantage, Art and the association membership benefited from an above average number of technical colleges compared to other regions and had developed proactive mutually beneficial relationships with college administrators over the years.

The association board, along with the colleges, recognized the growing challenge in front of them, but also saw an opportunity to tell the story about the benefits of careers in trades for young people.

Following several weeks of consultation with a variety of stakeholders, the association and colleges agreed to make the worthwhile investment in a joint storytelling campaign to showcase careers in trades. Combining the media networks of the colleges and the association provided considerable reach and distribution of their content, which is anchored in a series of short videos where youth took a starring role, getting hands-on experience. Supported by an array of other content that was covered in previous chapters, the overall storytelling campaign was overseen by the association's marketing team with out-of-house video production and graphic design. The investment of time, energy, and money was meaningful, and the group had to prove to those ultimately funding the campaign (association members, colleges) that telling the story of careers in culinary arts was good for business. The goal: get more youth (17–24) to enroll in post-secondary institutions that specialize in culinary arts and design, striving for a 25% increase within 24 months. With that tangible increase in graduating students, the colleges would see their revenues increase with more students and the association members would have an increased flow of work-ready and trained chefs and support staff ready to meet the growing demand from the hospitality industry. I should note, telling the stories of these businesses is just one part of the overall journey.

In addition to the storytelling campaign, the association had developed an exciting and enticing recruitment and retainment strategy to ensure the newly trained students stayed once they arrived on site.

While the recruitment strategy is not necessarily directly tied to storytelling for business, remember that storytelling for business always serves a purpose. For the hospitality association, it's to get more youth trained and on the job; for the colleges, it's to get more kids interested in getting culinary training at their institutions. When developing your storytelling for business plan as discussed in Chapter 3, "Build your own media network", work with everyone involved to discuss what can actually happen when storytelling works. I have this discussion with all my clients at the onset of every storytelling campaign as I want them to maximize the return on their investment and not miss the opportunity of increased business or the realization of any other objective. I've witnessed too many companies that are simply not prepared when new business arrives. For example, not hiring extra staff or securing the necessary resources when the extra sales and leads arrive because of harnessing the power of storytelling for business.

A look ahead

Chapter 10 is all about the crucial importance of measuring your storytelling for business campaigns, and I'll refer back to the case study throughout the chapter to demonstrate how Art and his team monitored and measured the success of his campaign. Moreover, we explain some of the leading benchmarks and tools to measure if your storytelling succeeded in supporting the goals of the organization, and how you can leverage them to track ROI. And, then once you have the data you need, I will share what to do with it next to maximize your storytelling for business investment.

If you aim for nothing, you're sure to hit it

If you aim for nothing, you're sure to hit it, as the famous quote intimates from those who've expressed it in various iterations, and this saying is as equally important when it comes to measurement of your storytelling for business projects. However, as even the most experienced business storyteller will tell you, present company included, measurement of storytelling is not always an easy endeavour. Most formal and informal communications surveys consistently show that measurement is one area storytellers need the most help with.[1] That's not to say over the years there hasn't been some meaningful and worthwhile progress made. For example, in 2010, some 200 of the world's leading public relations and communications delegates gathered in Barcelona to develop the oft-cited and aptly titled Barcelona Principles to create the first overarching framework for measurement.[2] The principles have undergone some updates over the years, but chief among them are goal setting and measurement, which are fundamental to communication and public relations. Measurement and evaluation require both qualitative and quantitative methods, which we'll cover in greater detail throughout this chapter.

Moreover, as you've discovered in building your own media network, the data that online platforms produce can be informative, insightful, and at the same time, somewhat overwhelming. Business storytellers now have more qualitative data quite literally at their fingertips than they ever have before. The challenge with this embarrassment of riches is determining what data best aligns to the objective of your storytelling for business. For Art and his hospitality association, they need the appropriate data to measure if their storytelling campaign succeeded in getting more youth enrolling in culinary technical colleges.

No matter when you start, it's paramount you measure in support of the goals and objectives of your business. Too many business storytellers too often develop measurements independent of what the business is trying to achieve. As part of your planning, set aside time at the start to assess what metrics matter most for measurement based on the strategic plan or business plan, and if a few rank higher than others, then assigning a greater weighted proportion of measurement serves as an excellent method to establishing a rate card of measurement for your storytelling endeavours. For example, in Art's case, he wanted his industry to be first in the market for youth to consider for a career over others, and he employed storytelling to get their attention. Given the importance of meeting his members' need to recruit new students, Art's hospitality association needed data to ensure the campaign was working. This chapter will guide how you develop, produce, and measure the success of the storytelling content, much like it did for Art and the hospitality association. For now, I'll cover some of the foundational metrics to strongly consider as you measure your objectives of your story for business.

Output and outcomes

Most of this chapter covers some essential data benchmarks for business storytellers, but before assessing and determining how to measure storytelling success, take some time to assess what your measurement means in relation to monitoring.

Output-based objectives measure against the volume of engagements with your channels of communication within your own media network. For example, how many people visited your website or downloaded your report or white paper as a result of engaging with the story of your business? Outcome-based objectives measures what happens after your stakeholders interact with your story. For example, what did your audience do as a result of interacting with your story? Did awareness of your product or service increase by 25% over a determined period of time? Did you influence your audience to take a specific action with a specific target, such as increase enrollment by 30% in your online courses?

Get SMART

While we're reviewing meaningful measurement monitoring, it's always worth another review of the tried-and-true SMART criteria many successful storytellers embrace when assessing the success of their content. Over the decades, many nuances within the criteria have been developed, and I encourage you to explore the definitions that work best for your storytelling. For example, some businesses define the "A" as attainable or assignable. For *Storytelling for Business*, SMART looks like this:

> **Specific** – What specifically do you want your story to achieve?
> **Measurable** – What specifically will your story measure?
> **Achievable** – Is the story's objective realistic, considering the time and resources required?
> **Relevant** – Is the story relevant to what your stakeholders need? For example, does your story help solve a problem or answer nagging questions?
> **Time-bound** – How long does your storytelling campaign last to achieve its objectives?

Paid, owned, and earned

Restating, the need for storytelling covers a lot of rationale, and for the sake of review in the context of measurement, some of the more common objectives include generating sales or sales leads, building brand awareness, educating, and influencing an audience to do something or creating a heightened sense of trust among your stakeholders. For the hospitality association in the opening case study, generating "leads" for the colleges to train more young people for careers in the hospitality industry, and influencing those young people to make the choice to invest in a career in culinary arts will indeed be a worthwhile decision.

Business storytelling initiatives like the hospitality association's measure and monitor the success of their effort in three industry-recognized streams: owned, earned, and paid media.

Owned media

The storytelling content you produce, either in-house or with the support of out-of-house agencies, is owned by your business, and therefore is known as owned media. It is the content you've produced that is distinct to your business, distributed on your own media network.

Earned media

Also known as advertising value equivalent (AVE), earned media is the measurement of the content output as covered or reported by the mainstream media's network. For example, with the hospitality association, as part of its storytelling, the team engaged the mainstream media with fun and interactive challenges with members of the news media. On a recent publicity blitz, morning show hosts were invited to one of the member technical colleges to try their hand at some culinary trades. The publicity is influential as it's reaching young people and their parents, who will most likely pay their tuition, and the editorial coverage doesn't cost the campaign any advertising dollars. Yet, calculating the amount of editorial airtime that the publicity garnered is still measuring in advertising rates, thus giving you an earned media metric. Furthermore, additional social metrics including engagements and impressions (covered later in this chapter) are converted into metrics that further establish a return on investment. Simply put, the campaign earned the media coverage without having to pay for it with traditional advertising dollars, yet the value of that "free" media is still calculated as part of the overall measurement of the campaign's storytelling for business.

While we're discussing earned media, it's important to share with you that the mainstream media are hyper-aware of when they're being exploited for publicity. Remember: treat any storytelling via publicity with the media as a partnership, and you will yield better results. For the morning show producers, they're always looking for content that's interactive for live television. They'll "trade" the free airtime on their morning shows in exchange for informative and visual content that their hosts can participate in, and which their audiences will find interesting. The hospitality association scored some significant earned mainstream media as they created a live story the morning show found compelling to share as well.

One caveat about earned media/AVEs to consider is just how reliable this key performance indicator (KPI) really is when one considers the size and scope of data that can be harvested. Some questions to consider: how is the quality of coverage truly assessed or the context of the feedback as it relates to the story? Accordingly, reporting may be out of proportion to reality. Earlier, we referenced the Barcelona Principles 2.0 report. In it, the authors of the report suggest not using AVEs at all, instead use negotiated advertising rates and consider the quality of coverage, including negative results.[3] Regardless of the industry's perspective, or your own as a storyteller, the fact remains earned media and AVEs are still of perceived value to many leaders, marketing professionals, and support stakeholders. As storytellers leading the measurement of content, it's up to us to educate and provide direction on what KPIs truly reflect the value of the storytelling.

Paid media

As you might expect, paid media is what you directly pay for to guarantee your story will receive exposure with the mainstream media and on social media platforms. In regards to influencing teens to consider careers in the culinary trade, the hospitality association complemented its owned media with paid media in high-traffic areas where they knew students would see them, which included social media advertising (YouTube, Twitter spots), along with digital billboards in areas documented to be seen by teens at a high volume. In addition to guaranteeing exposure, the benefit of paid media for business storytellers is that the investment includes comprehensive reporting to document your return on advertising with their platforms, and if they don't, you may want to consider other paid media that includes how your money was spent and what return you're getting for your investment.

Measuring up measurements

As with so many aspects of social media, when it comes to the data online platforms produce, the paradox of choice is staggering, and at times, incredibly intimidating, but it doesn't have to be if you start with some of the industry-standard measurements. And, as you get more comfortable, dive deeper into the ocean of metrics that are at your disposal. Some business storytellers create their own formulas, weighting importance based on the priority objectives of the storytelling campaign and/or the organization itself.

Social engagement

Take a moment and think about some of the stories you've recently consumed on social media. Perhaps the content succeeded in leading you to a call-to-action or influenced you to do something you previously hadn't considered. How did you express your appreciation or disapproval? For most of us, we engage with the social media platform by "liking" or sharing, or re-posting on our own social channels, or simply just having a look. Furthermore, we could comment on the storytelling content. Whatever you choose to do with that story, you've engaged with that content, and for measurement purposes, that is called engagement. Just about every social media platform has robust engagement metrics and is generally considered lead metrics for storytelling measurement.

Impressions

How many times your content is shown on a social media platform, regardless of whether your audience chooses to engage with it or not, is known as impressions, and is considered a staple social media metric. As your business gets introduced to social media metrics, you may be more than happy with just impressions, or as you get more sophisticated and experienced (and it doesn't take long once you get going), you may prefer engagements over impressions or a combination of both, as was the case for the trades association in developing is objectives for measurements. While the trades storytelling team valued impressions, and gave it some weight, they placed greater weight on engagements as they needed to know their stories resonated with their younger and fickle audience.

Reach

Think about your own social media habits and the hours of content you scroll through, consuming many stories, but never stopping to engage with them. Either way, that storytelling content has reached you as a unique user on social media. A unique user is a term referenced as a term of measurement for both website and social media metrics. A unique user is someone who visits your platform, regardless of how many times they are tracked during visits. The more unique users give you greater context of how many people are consuming the storytelling for your business.

Share of voice (SOV)

For the hospitality association, their plight of getting young people into jobs offered by their members was certainly a scenario not unique to their industry. The hospitality industry and computer sciences sectors (just two examples) are also competing for the same heavily desirable demographic of young adults. As part of their measurement objectives, the storytelling efforts of the hospitality industry set a target of being a leader among their "competitors" when it comes to telling their story to entice and recruit young people into programs that train them to work in restaurants and the food preparation. Share of voice (SOV) is particularly useful for businesses or organizations as it helps them determine how their contents stack up against their competitors' messages and storytelling tools and tactics. My experience with SOV has proven especially helpful in understanding why, how, and when some unknown competitor is providing some challenges that were not initially considered, while at the same time learning where their content might be succeeding in contrast.

Tags (#hashtags and handles)

Of the many things social media platforms do extremely well is making measurement (more) accessible in its ability to instantaneously track storytelling content. In addition to the actual content, like a video, creating tags and referring your own media network's social handles when posting your video aids in the distribution of your storytelling. For the hospitality association, getting their target stakeholders to "endorse" the campaign by sharing its tags and messages, or writing something organically on their own was a key objective. Tracking and filtering tags, along with the association's social media handles, is data that's easily curated by social media platforms, and some of the most recognizable signposts that your desired stakeholders are responding to your storytelling content. As is the nature of social media, keep an eye out for organic tags created outside of your network, but that are still supportive of your campaign, and engage with them to increase the reach of your storytelling.

Sentiment

Measuring the sentimental response of your story for business falls most commonly into three categories: positive, neutral, and negative. Sentiment has grown in its popularity for social media measurement largely because it's easy to communicate. People either like, dislike, or have no real opinion about your story. For business storytellers whose leaders may not be the most socially savvy, sentiment is digestible as it's easily understood. While sentiment has its merit, my counsel always is not to lean on it too heavily for storytelling ROI or measurement, instead using it as part of a mix of metrics included in this chapter. Sentiment is certainly recognizable, but it's not always accurate, especially if your story generates hundreds, thousands, and maybe even millions of engagements. Yes, robust online social media monitoring programs exist, and we'll get into that a bit more later in the chapter, but accuracy challenges with sentiment also exist. If your storytelling campaign produces a considerable amount of sentiment data, consider pulling a healthy, yet reasonable sample size, and double-check for accuracy.

Furthermore, much like creating styles for your company's style guide or setting custom weighted measurements specific to your brand, monitoring a created subset of words for sentiment is a good strategy to provide greater context for sentimental response.

Website engagement

As you read in Chapter 4, "Choose your channel", your website is your anchor storytelling tool. And according to a 2020 Content Marketing Institute report, *Benchmarks, Budgets, and Trends*, most content marketers also rated their websites as one of their top tools for content marketing measurement, coming in at number two (read further for number one).[4] In addition to its immense capacity to tell, showcase, and archive stories, your website has the enormous ability to provide rich and insightful data about how visitors to your website engage with your storytelling content.

Major search engine companies, most notably Google, have created online resources for you to track visitors to your website. Google Analytics, by way of example, provides you with a unique identification number that's embedded into the code of your websites, which enables a mindboggling dashboard of website monitoring data for you to explore. As it relates to the story of your business, and how you're positioning your content across your website, Google Analytics shows you key measurables such as time spent consuming your storytelling content, what content they prefer, where your visitors are from, along with clicks, downloads, and so much more. By design, *Storytelling for Business* is here to simply introduce you to the richness of website dashboards, which are an absolute essential to any measurement component of your storytelling for business campaign, much as they were for Art and his hospitality association. They needed to know that when their audience landed on their website to get more information, measuring the number of click-throughs to their partnering technical colleges was crucial data to measure if their storytelling was working.

Email engagement

As referenced earlier, content marketers, according to the 2020 Content Marketing Institute (CMI) study, rank their websites as number two on their top five metrics to measure performance. Apologies for leaving you hanging, the number one measuring metric according to the study is email engagement. In previous chapters, we explored what makes email newsletter programs impactful and that includes their ability to harness how users are engaging with the storytelling content.

Some key email metrics include whether your email list subscribers open your email (open rate), and if they do, whether they click any of your storytelling links to videos or webpage stories (click-through rate). Related, the conversion rate measures the percentage of those who did what you wanted them to do, such as consume your storytelling content. Some email programs also track forwarding (forwarding rate), which is important to gauge if you audience feels the stories of your business are worth sharing.

Speaking of open rates, in 2019, one of the leading email newsletter programs measured the average open rates for companies of all sizes with lists of 1,000+ subscribers that use its platform. Its data shows the average open rate for all industries is 21.33.[5] However, given the enormous increase in content production and the competition for people to consume it, the average open rate remains open to debate.

Depending on if a storytelling metric is to grow your email list, then certainly the number of new subscribers is an objective; conversely, if you measure a noticeable amount of unsubscribers, then your content may be doing the opposite of engaging your audience.

Do it with data

If you've found yourself reticent to dive into the data your storytelling platforms offer, you're not only missing out on setting and measuring KPIs, but also losing out on some valuable insight that can make your storytelling for your business better, as we've discussed in this chapter. In addition to the data and metrics built right into most platforms, a number of other independent measurement options exist assist you with your KPI storytelling benchmarks.

Sensational surveys!

Online surveys are easy to access and generally even easier to create. Enter "online survey tools" (or something similar) to see a wide range of platforms that poll your audience about the stories of your business. Most, if not all, of the survey programs start you off with a free edition, requesting payment either after a trial period has lapsed or if you require the benefits more data reporting features. As this is a chapter about making measurement matter, online surveys provide you with one of the best measurement methods to truly gauge your customers' engagement with your stories but also what your stories are designed to do – whether that's sell a product, influence people to do something or other call to action. Of all the measurement platforms covered in this chapter, online survey tools remain one of the most robust for its data curation, analysis, and reporting.

Focus groups

Focus groups can fall into one of two categories – formal and informal. Formal focus groups tend to be led by a facilitator who interviews selected members or segments of your audience for the sole purpose of gathering valuable insight and analysis about your business, and for the purpose of storytelling for business, to assess if you're getting a return on your storytelling investment. Focus groups work well as they can provide you direct access to your customers and in many cases, you can even watch and listen to the proceedings live, if that's the set up you choose with an agency that facilitates that kind of meeting space. Formal focus groups can be pricey as they require, in most cases, retaining an out-of-house agency, which is certainly worthwhile if your storytelling is a major thrust of your business at an advanced level and budget. Don't fret though if you're a smaller business as you can still reap the benefits of surveys with informal focus groups, which can include interviewing your customers with brief surveys as they enter/exit your business or invitations to take online surveys (when they have time) as just two examples.

Tools of the trade

As we near the end of *Storytelling for Business*, my sincere intention is that by now, you've learned about the industry standard tools and technologies to tell the story of your business, and the other options that go beyond this book, which I hope I've piqued your curiosity to explore further. As identified in this and previous chapters, the tools exist for your benefit, and furthermore, technology and platforms exist to manage and monitor your storytelling efforts.

Media monitoring

The level at which you invest in media monitoring services to capture media coverage or references of the story of your business often correlates to the scope and size of your storytelling endeavours. In your favourite search engine, simply enter "media monitoring" and a range of platforms and services will be available to you. These programs, much like social media platforms, pack a punch when it comes to reporting data and metrics. For companies that have a notable presence with their own media network, having a second set of "eyes" on the internet is not only a worthwhile investment it's an absolute must as shared in Chapter 8, "When a story goes sideways". Depending on how you set your platform up, you can receive up-to-the-second reports on any story you tell, followed up by detailed dashboard data reports. For smaller businesses, just a forewarning, these platforms are expensive, even at the entry level, but for good reason considering the 24/7 monitoring and in-depth monitoring services. If you choose to engage in a lot of storytelling and want the tracking, but are low on budget, I've worked with some business communicators that have pooled their budgets to pay for the service as they know making measurement matters. If your storytelling is modest, and can be tracked as needed, with search engine searches or browser alerts, plus the other metrics covered in this chapter, it's a worthwhile place to start.

Social listening

Very similar to media monitoring services, social listening platforms are worth exploring. Also known as social media aggregators, they allow you to manage all your social accounts in your media network through one platform, depending on the level of service you choose, these platforms come with both media monitoring and social listening capabilities. I've yet to work with a social media manager who doesn't have access to a platform that tracks how their content is being received. Related, many out-of-house social media agency options exist if your business needs the data, insight, and monitoring on campaign-by-campaign basis, which again is a good idea as they are generally expensive for smaller companies, plus they require considerable amount of extra work to customize to your business to measure and monitor your content, most definitely when it comes to measuring sentiment. If you don't have the budget and the time, starting with an out-of-house option will offer your business an informative entry point into the world of social listening.

Don't get me wrong, I'm a big fan of social media monitoring platforms as I'm using a couple myself currently, but my experience, and that of experienced social media managers in my network, is when it comes to sentiment, have realistic expectations. The data dump you often get back may not always be reliable and I have known many social strategists who spend countless hours confirming the sentiment is indeed truly accurate to the social media post.

CRMs

As noted, many social media listening platforms come bundled with media monitoring, and if you haven't checked yet, investigate what options exist with your customer relationship manager (CRM) if you use one, and most businesses do. A CRM's primary function is to track your relationship with your clients and customers, but just like other online platforms, there are many to choose from. When selecting a CRM platform, consider what features it offers to measure storytelling content, as many of the leading CRM companies do. As competition increases for customer retention, more CRM platforms have incorporated new options that facilitate storytelling, including email marketing and the ability to post and share content, both internally and externally.

Onside with online services

If you're serious about storytelling for business or you're just about to get serious, as you've read this far into the book, then at some point you'll also need to invest in some level of online social or media monitoring service. The internet's landscape is infinite, taking more social space by the second, making the task to take it on yourself more challenging as your storytelling projects expand with it. Even if the storytelling of your business is mainstream media focused, all their editorial and coverage is posted and shared online, providing yet another incentive to invest in online monitoring as measurement does indeed matter.

Data danger

Whatever data and platforms you use to determine storytelling success covered in this chapter, some caveats are worth considering and revisiting. As shared earlier, the first is to ensure your data correlates specifically with your storytelling objectives that in turn, support the goals and objectives of the business. In many measurements, simply getting high engagement stats is the objective, but does that mean your story achieved the outcomes and outputs examined earlier in this chapter? If your data can't answer that question, you'll have to re-examine how your curated data supports your intended result, such as increased sales of a product or service.

The second caveat of data danger is to place too much emphasis on data that supports return on investment. That may seem somewhat contradictory to this chapter's content, but I've always viewed impactful storytelling as living somewhere near the middle on a content continuum between creativity and ROI. Meaning, the story of your business is produced with creativity to entertain and captivate your audience, but at the same time includes a narrative to influence them to do something to support your storytelling return on investment. For example, tell a clever story with real people in a visual setting that shows how your product solves a problem or fulfills a need, leaving your audience wanting to purchase or explore calls-to-action to learn more. But if your story goes too far to one end of the continuum it may be fun to watch, but does it sell any products? Or, if your story focuses too much on selling, it may be bogged down in information and disengage your audience.

The third caveat is that sometimes the story of your business can't or simply doesn't need to be measured where the outcome is to enhance the experience your audiences have with your brand so they continue to interact with your content. For example, for many businesses, keeping in regular contact with their audiences is done simply through consistent social posts and short videos, which many sports teams employ to keep their fans connected to their favourite teams and players. Having a coach talk about how they won the big game may not show direct ROI to selling products, but it does engage fans to interact with storytelling that is directly sales-oriented because they've built trust through previous content that doesn't just sell.

And a fourth caveat, for good measure, is to consistently analyze your measurement metrics. Are they still relevant or have other tools with advanced artificial intelligence come along, making what you currently rely on outdated in the face of new technology?

Share the wealth

As this chapter illustrates, a wealth of valuable measurement data is at your fingertips. No matter how large or small a selection of KPIs you establish, share the wealth with your necessary business stakeholders and leaders. Nothing creates greater investment in business storytelling than metrics that demonstrate a return on investment or even an attempted return on investment. Sometimes a storytelling campaign that doesn't succeed as intended can yield as much or even more valuable insight than if it had succeeded. Experienced and innovative business leaders are most often risk takers, appreciating that when storytelling doesn't produce the desired KPIs, there are valuable reasons why to learn from that serve the overall growth of the business. When sharing your measurement data, understand that not every stakeholder may grasp the same level of storytelling measurement jargon that you as a storyteller possess. When sharing your data, either educate what the definitions or data means or create your own language to make reading and understanding the reporting easier.

Worth repeating

Case study: Building a case for measurement

- Remember how Art and his association needed storytelling data to guide their strategy and determine what was working and not working
- Learn how Art wanted to know if the storytelling was reaching the desired demographics and want action they were taking after consuming the content

If you aim for nothing, you're sure to hit it

- Understand that connecting your storytelling objectives to that of your organization's objective remains a top priority
- Without setting appropriate storytelling objectives, you're likely going to miss your target

Output and outcomes

- Use output measurement to assess engagement metrics, such as website visits
- Use outcome measurement to assess what people did as a result of visiting your website

Get SMART

- **Specific** – What specifically do you want your story to achieve?
- **Measurable** – What specifically will your story measure?
- **Achievable** – Is the story's objectives realistic, taking into account the time and resources required?
- **Relevant** – Is the story relevant to what your stakeholders need? For example, does your story help solve a problem or answer nagging questions?
- **Time-bound** – How long does your storytelling campaign last to achieve its objectives?

Paid, owned, and earned

- **Owned media:** The storytelling content you produce
- **Earned media:** Also known as Advertising Value Equivalent (AVE), earned media is the measurement of the content output as covered or reported by mainstream media, keeping in mind this metric while well-recognized, should be scrutinized in your storytelling measurement
- **Paid media:** directly pay for to guarantee your story will receive exposure with the mainstream media and on social media platforms

Measuring up measurements

Engagement KPIs include:

- Impressions
- Reach
- Share of voice (SOV)
- Tags (#hashtags and handles)
- Sentiment
- Website engagement
- Email engagement

Do it with data

- Try surveys which are generally accessible for use with a variety of online platforms
- Use focus groups when more in-depth research and insight is necessary

Tools of the trade

- Online platforms effective for collecting and analyzing storytelling data include: media monitoring, social listening, and customer relationship management (CRM) programs

Data danger

- Assess that the data you collect is in alignment with your storytelling objectives
- Avoid excessive emphasis of ROI on your data's results; sometime data doesn't tell the entire story exclusively

Share the wealth

- Share your data with everyone who needs to see the metrics, allowing them to understand the benefits of storytelling for business
- Create reporting language and dashboard that are easily understood

11

The stories you tell yourself

Case study: Storytelling to the rescue

Any CPR is better than no CPR. That was a saying I heard often among instructors who taught people about how to administer the lifesaving technique properly, providing them the best chance to save someone's life. For many countries, the bigger challenge remains that getting people motivated to take the training and to understand they are protected by law in most jurisdictions if the attempt to use CPR and/or an AED is unsuccessful.

One of my first storytelling roles as a communicator was working for the Canadian Red Cross and one of my annual storytelling projects was to increase the awareness of the need to get trained in CPR and AED. Ask anyone who has used their CPR and AED training, and I have many times through interviews, and they'll tell you it is an incredibly emotional experience, expressing their gratitude for the training when they needed it most.

They've shared that even though their emotions were running extremely high, their training kicked in "by instinct" and they knew how to get started with CPR, while taking the necessary steps to secure an AED that was available nearby. As you can also imagine for the person who has survived because of someone administering CPR and AED training, it's an emotional experience as well. And that's the powerful story that we leveraged to explain how everyday people were thrust into a lifesaving situation when they least expected it. Storytelling to the rescue, so to speak.

With permission, discretion, and sensitivity, we reconnected the person who was rescued with their rescuer, who was nominated to receive a Red Cross Rescuer Award at an annual ceremony. The criteria for the award also included rescue attempts that were not successful, as communicating the courage to take the training and use it was commendable regardless of the outcome. Along with their families, local dignitaries, special guests, and the media were also invited to amplify the message for training. Content was also captured and distributed nationally on the social media channels and websites belonging to the Canadian Red Cross. In most cases, the awards were presented directly by the people who were rescued to the people who rescued them, with very few dry eyes in the room when each side shared their intensely emotional story. In fact, I'm getting teary-eyed simply recalling their stories and the response from the room. The ceremonies were an opportunity to express gratitude, underscoring with real-life examples the need to get CPR and AED training and that it works. Though, despite best attempts and data that shows that it works, providing CPR and using an AED, does not always work in every situation.

With extraordinary humility, one person shared her immense gratitude by presenting a Red Cross Rescuer Award to another person who used all his training to the best of his ability, but ultimately, the training and use of the AED was not enough. Nonetheless, if you lost a loved one to cardiac arrest, even if they didn't pull through, knowing someone was there to attempt to save their life provides comfort and solace, as was shared by some who had lost loved ones in this circumstance.

The measured earned and owned media key performance indicators (KPIs) from this campaign were significant, generating multiple stories and features, plus additional editorial opportunities that showcased, through human connection, the need to get CPR and AED training, and that you are protected by law if you are not successful in your rescue attempt. Furthermore, the content on the society's own channels of communication was shared nationally, generating reach and impact with an overwhelmingly positive sentiment. As shared in Chapter 6, "People power", working with real people to tell this story was the most impactful and meaningful strategy to connect with the public to influence them to get trained in CPR and AED. Most importantly, this storytelling initiative generated an increased interest in the number of people who wanted to be trained in CPR and the proper use of an AED.

In the introduction of *Storytelling for Business*, I shared my rationale for not using real names or organizations in my chapter case studies but have made an exception for this final chapter with permission from the Canadian Red Cross to encourage you and others to invest in CPR and AED training. Please visit www.redcross.ca/AED

Furthermore, this real-life case study emphasizes the power of storytelling, and that storytelling is not only effective, but rewarding for the storyteller, both personally and professionally. As a journalist, content creator, and communicator, what I've shared in *Storytelling for Business* has guided me through thousands of stories I have had the good fortune to be a part of, successes and failures. In addition to providing you with chapters to serve as storytelling resources, I felt compelled to have the last chapter include the stories I told myself as I navigated some remarkable and memorable storytelling challenges, both good and bad.

A look ahead

Chapter 11 reveals that storytelling for business is not always an easy journey, but certainly worth taking the risk as the benefits can be profound and rewarding, both personally and professionally. Hence the rationale for including the Canadian Red Cross case study. This final chapter in *Storytelling for Business* provides some guidance and advice on maintaining storytelling perseverance and focus in the face of some detractors who may try to knock you back.

Not for the faint of heart

One of the largest criticisms levelled against social media is that many of their users choose to hide their identity on various platforms and then use that anonymity to express (mostly) negative comments and opinions. I call this "virtual courage". Sharing one's own opinion is fine, but the criticism of social media cuts sharper when those opinions and comments turn to vitriol, spewing incorrect, hurtful, or damaging information for whatever reason. I'm never quite sure what motivates people to "express" opinions in such a manner they never would if they were standing face-to-face with that person. Again, virtual courage. However, this reality exists and is ever-present with storytelling for business, and if you're sensitive to criticism on social media, warranted or not, take it as fair warning that storytelling is not always for the faint of heart.

My storytelling experience includes serving as a communications and content lead for a leading North American sports and entertainment company. The overwhelming majority of my storytelling experiences during my time at the company remain among some of my career highlights, but along the way, I have been personally trolled and criticized on my social media platforms or witnessed users take the "fire, ready, aim" approach when posting comment about our teams' or players' content. Reiterating, storytelling's not for the faint of heart or for those with "thin skin", but like many storytellers for business, trolling is just part of the territory, and social media does provide the opportunity for a much greater good.

I also kept tabs on how other sports teams managed the machinations of social media, and more clubs and their leaders are fighting back to make a point. Many (growing) examples exist, including Swansea soccer club, which took a seven-day social media hiatus in April 2021 to "battle against abuse and discrimination of all forms on our social media".[1]

To offer some context to the scope of cyberbullying, Facebook removed tens of millions of pieces of hate speech content from its platform annually from 2017 to 2021.[2] And even the mainstream media is not immune to "virtual courage", with many prominent news organizations choosing to limit the posting of comments or disabling the feature outright due to hateful discourse shared on their platforms.

Many industries, and the businesses within them, grapple with the social media paradox: use it to promote the story of their business to grow their business, but at the same time, risk facing punishing criticism and, at times, unfounded and discriminatory comments. The story I tell myself is producing content for online distribution is completely worth it, as storytelling, and the reach social media facilitates, has proven again and again that it's enormously effective, and certainly worth the risk.

An ounce of humility can save you a pound of pain

Throughout the storytelling process, creating checks and balances along the way, can save you a lot of time, effort, and resources. It's hard to genuinely ask, free of confirmation bias, "is the story of my business any good?" It's much harder to pull your story campaign back or shelve it altogether if your story goes sideways, as we covered in Chapter 8. With an ounce of humility, you'll save yourself a pound of pain if you're open to listening and accepting feedback.

Unfortunately, or fortunately, depending on your perspective, making a mistake (hopefully not too often) is a good teacher for business storytelling. Early in my career, I worked with an organization where one of the leaders insisted on a specific message in what was a high-profile campaign. With humility, I reflect now on not seeking more to understand, choosing instead to use my influence to advance my preference in messaging and not use his. Suffice it to say, when the storytelling rolled out, it was evident very quickly that the leader's message would have been much better suited, and I have learned ever since to remain very cognizant of other points of view.

Listen to that inner voice

I once had a news director tell me when it came to making difficult editorial decisions, trust your instinct because sometimes that's all you have. Never have wiser words been shared with me. With some storytelling initiatives, whether it's just before sending out a media release, posting a video on social media, or scheduling a media conference where that inner voice said, "you may just want to check it one more time or you may just want to hold off", and where I've listened, I was grateful and when I ignored that inner counsel, I either paid the price with the online commentariat or had a very close call. Don't forget about your Touchstone Team, introduced to you in Chapter 8. When your inner voice is drowned out by too much external "noise", that team will prove invaluable.

Sometimes your critics are right

For many storytellers, one of the hardest things to hear is you got something wrong, and I'd extend that sentiment to business storytellers. A fair amount of time, effort, and resources goes into storytelling for business, and the more a company invests in telling their story, the higher the stakes if a story goes sideways – a true escalation of commitment. With humility comes the responsibility to your business and to yourself as a business storyteller to reflect, as needed, to ask the question: "are they right, did we get something wrong?" I'm not suggesting you stop or pivot your entire storytelling campaign over a few fervent negative comments on social platforms, but if the "noise" is too loud to "hear" anything else, and it's having an impact on your operations or rapidly eroding your company's goodwill, I assure you, you'll know, and action will be required. Chapter 8 covered some strategies and tactics to manage when a story goes sideways, whereas the story I've told myself over the years is that as hard as it is to go through, there will always be a silver lining, and that is some beneficial level of learning from the mistake. At every point along my storytelling journey, whether in senior-level editorial positions or in senior-level communications positions, learning from mistakes creates opportunities to tell stories or manage risk better than was done previously. The biggest challenge you and your business may face is whether you have the courage to ask the tough questions.

No reward without some risk

As shared in the opening case study of the Red Cross Rescuer Awards, the outcome met objectives, created compelling content, and influenced people to take action to pursue CPR and AED training. This was certainly not without risk, as anytime you put that much unfiltered human emotion on display, live in front of an audience, and with the media capturing every moment, the story could have gone sideways, and in our planning, we covered every conceivable "detour" and how we'd manage it. With a plan, we proceeded, and it was well worth the risk to tell a truly memorable and remarkable story.

You can't make everyone happy – accept it

If you're going to tell the story of your business, at some point, you're going to have to make some decisions or simply choose to get started in the first place. Borrowing from Theodore Roosevelt's oft cited *Man in the Arena* speech: "The credit belongs to the man who is actually in the arena, whose face is marred by dust and sweat and blood; who strives valiantly; who errs, who comes short again and again." Not to get too dramatic, and restating, that most of your storytelling will likely be free of sideway swerves; the point I'm emphasizing here is that successful business storytellers plan well, assess the risk, and then get in the arena.

In some storytelling scenarios, such as when your business has to promote new policies, but may be viewed as "inconvenient", invariably, detractors (as identified in Chapter 7, "Audience analysis") will likely surface to sharply criticize or attempt to mobilize others. Popular researcher and author Brené Brown colloquially refers to this common enabling as "invisible armies", pretending to represent others' opinions to form criticism from the "cheap seats".[3]

The hard storytelling truth is you simply can't make everyone happy – accept it. Recall Chapter 1's case study and the need to tell a story to support a challenging policy change. The response from stakeholders was difficult at first, but with some time the policy change was accepted on its merit – for the greater good. Sometimes you must tell difficult stories because not telling them will bring greater harm to your business.

You can't have it both ways

The last story I recommend storytellers tell their leaders and other internal stakeholders who want the benefit of storytelling, but not the risk associated with it, is you can't have it both ways. Storytelling for business has become the lead communication and marketing tool for countless companies because it works and achieves and supports objectives to grow businesses. Remember Dan from Chapter 6's "People power"? As the face and voice of the organization, all stakeholders benefited from his influence and celebrity to get things done. The same goes for Erick from Chapter 8's "When stories go sideways". Any time a leader goes live in front of an audience or the media, the risk for a story to go sideways will always be present – always. You can plan and consider every eventuality, but you can't plan for absolutely everything, and must ultimately decide whether it's worth getting into the arena. And, most importantly, before you do, know that key stakeholders support the storytelling when it's successful and when it goes sideways, need immediate action to get the narrative back on track.

Worth repeating

Case study: Storytelling to the rescue

- Learn from case study that centred around genuine human interest stories

- Set storytelling goals and objectives of getting more people interested and signed up for CPR and AED training

Not for the faint of heart

- Understand that not all storytelling is easy
- Expect, at times, for intense pushback, both for your business and the lead storytellers
- Know that you're not alone as most storytellers experience some level of "trolling"

An ounce of humility can save you a pound of pain

- Create checks and balances to ensure your storytelling is working

Listen to that inner voice

- Trust your storytelling instinct because often that's all you have to make (tough) decisions

Sometimes your critics are right

- Have the humility to accept feedback, even criticism, for the greater good of getting better and avoiding future mistakes

No reward without some risk

- Understand that while there will always be some level of risk with telling the story of your business, research and planning goes a long way in mitigating negative outcomes

You can't make everyone happy – accept it

- Accept that when it comes to telling your story, not everyone is going to like it – and that's okay

You can't have it both ways

- Understand that getting the benefits from the power of storytelling and not having a presence on your own media network are mutually exclusive

Conclusion

As I've come to understand and appreciate with the book writing process through research and conversations, many authors start and stop many times, and in many cases, don't finish at all. And now that I have stopped, started, and paused numerous times over the past ten years leading up to *Storytelling for Business* – wondering sometimes whether I'd ever finish writing a book at all – I completely get it, and applaud anyone who even gets into the arena, whether they finish or not. When it came time to write *Storytelling for Business*, I initially told no one at first. Eventually, I did tell my wife Lisa, giving her the rationale and explanation for all the 5am writing sessions, which occurred just outside our master bedroom in my home office. A few months in, and making progress, I told my two daughters. I guess I wanted them to see what the manifestation of what completing a major project looks like, and what goes into completing such an endeavour.

Frankly, the reason for my clandestine approach to writing this book was that I was insecure I wouldn't finish – again. Though I *just knew* this time was different, and it was, completing the draft of the book in just under nine months, writing every single week with the goal of writing, at minimum, five to ten pages. The editing and working with my publisher, Practical Inspiration, required additional weeks of work, but I remained committed as the end was always in sight. The key for me was *just don't stop,* and there were sure times when I wanted to, believe me. When I told my oldest, Livia, what I was up to, her immediate response was "what is your book about?". While I had created an outline and determined my "thesis" was storytelling for business, I hadn't actually yet contemplated the "why" for why anyone should read this book. Caught off-guard by the question, though up for the challenge of providing an answer – and forever grateful for the genuine inquisition – my response was almost immediate: "helping businesses tell stories that connect them with the people that matter most". I remember vividly holding my breath in suspension in that moment, captured in the intense grip of needing her affirmation.

That affirmation, on a broader scale, is also what drives me and many other business storytellers. We ultimately want the storytelling content we produce to *affirm* what we've set out to achieve, whether that's getting stakeholders to buy a product, invest in a service, or influence them into a desirable action. Though as shared in the previous chapter, if your business, or you as a storyteller, are open to it, opportunity is also found in affirmations not confirmed.

The practice of storytelling for business is a never-ending pursuit, and as variations of the adage go, the more you know the less you know. That became overwhelmingly, yet enthusiastically, abundantly clear that my journey continues – and continues with gratitude. And as much as the platforms that will make up your own media network change, evolve, or fade away, and as much as the technology comes and goes, along with the members of the mainstream media (and the outlets they work for), one constant will always remain – storytelling for business comes down to a great story. If you've made it this far into the book, I know you have it in you, or you're close to taking the next steps.

As for my daughter's response and how I answered her question about what is *Storytelling for Business* about, she genuinely replied,

"I get it, Dad. That's cool." Whew! Cool indeed! My teenage daughter got it, and that is my sincere intention for this book *Storytelling for Business: The Art and Science of Creating Connection in the Digital Age*, that you "get it", too.

I'd love to hear about the story of your business and if my journey has served you in any way. Please reach out to me through my website www.robwozny.com or message through the social media platforms on my own media network.

Acknowledgments

Storytelling for Business is here in the universe thanks to the inspiration and motivation blessed upon me by three special girls in my life – my best friend, life partner, and wife, Lisa, and our daughters, Livia and Jovan. While you gave me my space to create, your presence kept me going and sustained me in more ways than you can ever know. Thank you.

I simply could not write this book without the tremendous privilege and responsibility entrusted in me to tell the stories of some remarkable organizations over the years. To the leaders, clients, owners, and enablers who gave me the greatest of responsibilities and opportunities to tell their stories, this book is for you all.

As a journalist, the same sense of gratitude, except from the other side of the lens, so to speak, is extended to the thousands of people who I've interviewed to create hundreds of memorable stories, some of which shaped who I am as an overall storyteller and as a human being.

Thanks to the University of Winnipeg's Rhetoric, Writing, and Communications program (my major) and its Professional, Applied and Continuing Education (PACE) where I completed my studies in public relations and business management. An educational institution is only as good as the professors and instructors they invest in to guide and shape the storytellers of tomorrow. Along my journey, I was honoured to learn from some of the best educators who hold a superior grasp of prose and narrative, including Janice Freeman, along with the late, but never forgotten, Robert (Bob) Byrnes and Carl Radimer. Your gifts for communication and content live on in this book.

Thank you to Alison Jones and her talented (and patient!) team at Practical Inspiration Publishing. While in the middle of all the edits you pushed me to go further, the book turned out better than I ever could have imagined because of your commitment to excellence. Your superior knowledge of the publishing industry continues to serve me well. To my manuscript readers: Carol, Connie, Elaine, Jennifer, Kathryn, Kevin, Moira, Victoria, and Sonya, plus my technical advisors (John "JD" and Craig) in some chapters, your feedback and perspective confirmed or altered the course of numerous sections. As a result, readers of *Storytelling for Business* receive a better reading experience because of your time, interest, and caring.

On a personal note, thank you to my dear friends Jon ("Jimmy"), Patrick, Stephan, Kevin ("Chiefer"), and Greg, along with my steadfast champions, Alana, Carol, Moira, and Colleen, along with Ruth who answered every "911" call, and cheered me on during the writing process. To this group, the importance of your support and friendship cannot be overstated. Thank you.

About the author

For more than 25 years, storytelling has been at the core of everything Rob Wozny has accomplished professionally – as an intrepid senior journalist, creative content strategist, and proven business communicator.

Leveraging his passion and experience for storytelling, Rob works with organizations to understand their goals and align them creatively to storytelling strategies that connect their business to the people that matter most.

As a sought-after instructor, speaker, and author, Rob shares storytelling opportunities and challenges, drawing on decades of experience serving senior leaders and entrepreneurs across a variety of industries.

However, the most rewarding and ever-evolving narrative for Rob is the story of his family, with his partner Lisa of 25 years, and their two daughters. Some of their favourite chapters have been "written" from outdoor and travelling activities with many more on the horizon.

Endnotes

Chapter 1

1. "2022 Global Marketing Trends". Deloitte Insights, www2.deloitte.com/us/en/insights/topics/marketing-and-sales-operations/global-marketing-trends/2020/purpose-driven-companies.html
2. "Global Consumers Seek Companies That Care about Environmental Issues". Nielsen, 9 November 2018, www.nielsen.com/eu/en/insights/article/2018/global-consumers-seek-companies-that-care-about-environmental-issues
3. Stu McLaren, Membership Workshop, 26 April 2021. Webinar.
4. Jeff Walker, *Launch: An Internet Millionaire's Secret Formula to Sell Almost Anything Online, Build a Business You Love, and Live the Life of Your Dreams*. Morgan James Publishing, 2014.
5. "This Is WE Day". WE Charity, www.we.org/en-CA/we-stories/we-day/what-is-we-day-speeches-and-performances-with-celebrities-students-and-social-activists
6. "About WE Charity – WE Charity Foundation (WCF)". WCF, www.wecharity.org/about-we-charity/our-story

Chapter 2

1. Paul J. Zak, "Why Your Brain Loves Good Storytelling". Harvard Business Review, 28 October 2014, https://hbr.org/2014/10/why-your-brain-loves-good-storytelling
2. Future of StoryTelling. "Q&A With Professor of Neuroscience Uri Hasson". Medium, 10 January 2020, https://medium.com/future-of-storytelling/q-a-with-professor-of-neuroscience-uri-hasson-b57e23476fab
3. Simon Sinek, *Start with Why: How Great Leaders Inspire Everyone to Take Action*. Portfolio/Penguin, 2013.
4. Microsoft Canada. *Attention Spans: Consumer Insights*. Microsoft Canada, Spring 2015.
5. Content Marketing Institute and Marketing Profs. B2B Content Marketing 2020, Benchmarks, Budgets, and Trends North America. San Diego, USA, 2020.
6. Kenneth Burke. *A Grammar of Motives*. University of California Press, 1969.
7. Joseph Campbell, *The Hero with a Thousand Faces*. New World Library, 2008.

Chapter 3

1. Streamyard Summit, 26 April 2021. Webinar.

Chapter 4

1. "Demographics of Social Media Users and Adoption in the United States". Pew Research Center: Internet, Science & Tech, Pew Research Center, 23 November 2021, www.pewresearch.org/internet/fact-sheet/social-media
2. Canada's Population Estimates: Total Population, July 1, 2018. www150.statcan.gc.ca/n1/en/daily-quotidien/180927/dq180927c-eng.pdf?st=Cl_5dsaX

3. Government of Canada, Statistics Canada. Smartphone Use and Smartphone Habits by Gender and Age Group, Inactive, Government of Canada, Statistics Canada, 22 June 2021, www150.statcan.gc.ca/t1/tbl1/en/tv.action?pid=2210011501

4. Government of Canada, Statistics Canada. Smartphone Use and Smartphone Habits by Gender and Age Group, Inactive, Government of Canada, Statistics Canada, 22 June 2021, www150.statcan.gc.ca/t1/tbl1/en/tv.action?pid=2210011501

5. Janet Stewart, How to Make Live Online Training More Engaging, 3 December 2021. Webinar.

6. Kayla Carmicheal. "The Best Time to Send an Email [Research]". HubSpot Blog, 29 June 2021, https://blog.hubspot.com/marketing/best-time-to-send-email

7. Elisa Shearer, "Social Media Outpaces Print Newspapers in the US as a News Source". Pew Research Center, 27 August 2020, www.pewresearch.org/fact-tank/2018/12/10/social-media-outpaces-print-newspapers-in-the-u-s-as-a-news-source

8. Apple. Apple's Paper and Packaging Strategy. Apple USA, October 2017.

Chapter 5

1. Edelman Trust Barometer 2020. www.edelman.com/sites/g/files/aatuss191/files/2020-01/2020%20Edelman%20Trust%20Barometer%20Global%20Report_LIVE.pdf

2. "News Watchers Overwhelmingly Prefer Television, While Readers Prefer the Web". Pew Research Center's Journalism Project, 29 November 2018, www.journalism.org/2018/12/03/americans-still-prefer-watching-to-reading-the-news-and-mostly-still-through-television/pj_2018-12-03_read-watch-listen_0-03

3. Stop Paid Content on CBC, www.stoppaidcontentoncbc. ca/open-letter

Chapter 6

1. Edelman Trust Barometer 2020. www.edelman.com/ sites/g/files/aatuss191/files/2020-01/2020%20 Edelman%20Trust%20Barometer%20Global%20 Report_LIVE.pdf
2. "How Athletes 10X Sponsor Performance on Social". Opendorse, 28 April 2021, https://opendorse.com/blog/ sponsored-content-in-sports-2019

Chapter 8

1. Chip Heath and Dan Heath. *Decisive: How to Make Better Choices in Life and Work*. Random House Canada, 2013.

Chapter 9

1. IABC Research Foundation and Buck Consultants. Employee Engagement Survey, p. 6. IABC Research Foundation and Buck Consultants. USA, 2010.
2. IABC Research Foundation and Buck Consultants. Employee Engagement Survey, p. 8. IABC Research Foundation and Buck Consultants. USA, 2010.

Chapter 10

1. PR news. "Which Area Do Communicators Need the Most Help with? #Prnews". Twitter, Twitter, 13 November 2018, https://twitter.com/PRNews/ status/1062410759056035847

2. Launch of Barcelona Principles 2. p. 9. https://amecorg. com/wp-content/uploads/2019/11/Barcelona-Principles-2.pdf

3. Launch of Barcelona Principles 2. p. 14. https://amecorg. com/wp-content/uploads/2019/11/Barcelona-Principles-2.pdf

4. Content Marketing 2020. p.31. https:// contentmarketinginstitute.com/wp-content/ uploads/2019/10/2020_B2B_Research_Final.pdf

5. "Email Marketing Benchmarks". Mailchimp, https:// mailchimp.com/resources/email-marketing-benchmarks

Chapter 11

1. AFC, Swansea City. "Swansea City Has Chosen to Take a Club-Wide Stance in the Battle against Abuse and Discrimination of All Forms on Social Media". Twitter, 8 April 2021, https://twitter.com/swansofficial/ status/1380113189447286791

2. Statista Research Department. "Facebook Hate Speech Removal per Quarter 2021". Statista, 12 November 2021, www.statista.com/statistics/1013804/ facebook-hate-speech-content-deletion-quarter

3. Brené Brown, The Dare to Lead Glossary: Key Language, Skills, Tools, and Practices, 2018, https://daretolead. brenebrown.com/wp-content/uploads/2018/10/ Glossary-of-Key-Language-Skills-and-Tools-from-DTL. pdf

Index

EXCLUSIVE BONUS!
The Storytellers Circle

You will create greater connection with the people who matter the most to your business if you follow everything in *Storytelling for Business: The Art and Science of Creating Connection in the Digital Age.*

The book is just one tool in my storytelling "toolbox" to build an online community of passionate business storytellers.

I'd like to offer you more!

As a **thank-you** for buying this book, you get a year's subscription to the Storytellers' Circle – **FREE!**

- Watch livestream and webinar recordings with Rob and special guests
- Learn from other creative business storytelling experts
- Create connections from other storytellers of business – just like you
- Access bonus instructional videos to complement what you've learned in this book
- Benefit from additional tools, resources, and research archived in the Storytellers' Circle

All of this and so much more is waiting for you now in the Storytellers' Circle!
www.robwozny.com/storytellerscircle

Rob Wozny

STORYTELLING FOR BUSINESS

PROFESSIONAL SPEAKING . WORKSHOPS

Rob Wozny works with businesses and leaders to tell stories that connect with the people that matter most. As a sought-after speaker and trainer, Rob's presentations and training have guided many organizations across a variety of industries to identify compelling business stories and empower the right people to tell them.

Available for speaking engagements, training sessions, and one-on-one leadership coaching, connect with Rob Wozny at www.robwozny.com